How to Buy Stocks Online

Without a Broker
Step-By-Step Guidance
For All Experience Levels

BY

Michelle Price

A Modern Wealth Media Publication

New York

To the most important people in my life:

Mom, Dad, Sister, Niece

Contents

"An investment in knowledge
pays the best interest."

Benjamin Franklin

INTRODUCTION

Ask anybody about getting rich. More people understand how to get rich from playing the lottery than from investing in stocks. In fact, two of the top five ways people learn investing are by searching online and guessing.

People invest billions online. However, they do it without *really* knowing how to invest. Why? Investment books are either too simple, or they need a PhD to understand them.

We need books that teach more than the basics. At the same time, we don't need all of the complex techniques professionals use in order to be successful investors.

This middle ground needs a book.

Investors Put Money to Work

What if you found a machine that could create a twin for you. You could send your twin to your day job. Meanwhile, you would do what you loved for a living.

JOEY DREAMS OF THE DAY WHEN HIS MONEY WORKS FOR HIM.

Well, I have bad news. A Xerox machine for people doesn't exist. Investing in stocks, however, can simulate one.

It's a key reason why people invest. Investors aim to put their money to work for them, so that they don't have to work for their money.

This is Not Your Parents' Stock Market

Who hasn't heard "buy quality stocks, wait for them to rise over the long term, and then sell at a profit"?

It's still mostly true. However, the 1990's introduced new subtleties and pitfalls.

For example, let's look at the S&P 500 index. It acts like a "thermometer", tracking the health of the US stock market. It developed a split personality in mid-1990:

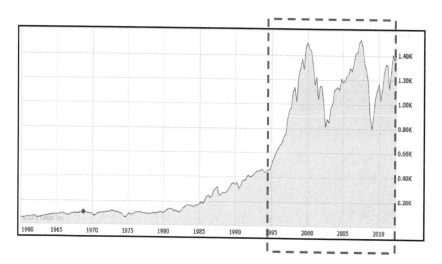

Notice how the market became an entirely different beast?!

The Digital Age Changed How Investors Invest

Investors started to have instant access to information on the internet in the mid-1990's. News flowed 24x7, allowing investors to react quickly to global events.

More institutions traded electronically to squeeze profits from buying and selling stocks after tiny price changes. This made the market choppy and volatile.

The US economy also experienced a tremendous expansion of economic activity, spurred by the boom in internet-based businesses.

Investors no longer had the luxury of time to ponder whether to buy or sell a stock. We said goodbye to the monochrome stock market, and entered a vibrant high-definition place. A place where the market's sensitivity to even a whiff of news increased.

The rules of trading changed. So must the advice.

My Promise with This Book

Many authors have never worked as professional investors. Other may have, yet talk at 1000 feet with anecdotes only they care about.

Until authors manage money, they can't write about the subtle points of investing. They also can't take the things professional investors know and translate them into language everyday investors understand.

The techniques I teach in this book are the same I used in the past to get a 300% return from stocks like Cephalon during a recession. They also helped me minimize losses in my clients' portfolios during the 2008 downturn.

You'll not only get a practical, step-by-step guide to buying stocks online, but you'll also get:

✓ Strategies to find opportunities to invest in the stock market, starting with using your common sense

✓ Rules on when to buy (and when to sell)

✓ Opinions on online discount brokers to help you find one best suited to your needs

I'll also fine tune your "gut" feeling for recognizing a good investment, and show you how to put together a portfolio to reach a goal.

YOU NEED HOPE AND A STRATEGY TO REACH YOUR GOALS.

Also in this book, we'll:

✓ Search for "value" investments. These stocks are "on sale", and appear underpriced in comparison to their actual value on paper.

✓ Create goal-based portfolios. We will figure out the types of stocks you need in your portfolio for it to grow to a target value. We'll also talk about how to minimize the risk of losing your money.

Most importantly, I'll try to talk in conversational language and not talk like we're at a snobby lecture. And no anecdotes – just the facts that you need to buy stocks online.

We all used training wheels before riding a bike. We all needed mom and dad to help us move from crawling to walking. Every investor needs a way to take his or her skills to the next level.

My hope is you will become a sharper, more successful investor after reading this book. I also hope you'll discover how investing can be exciting, a personal challenge, and even fun.

I'm honored you're reading "How to Buy Stocks Online" so I may be part of your journey to become a great investor.

Michelle Price

Managing Principal

Price Capital, LLC

Registered Investment Advisor and Financial Planner

Important Note

Buying stocks is not for everyone. Investing is at your own risk.

While I give opinions in this book, these opinions do not constitute investment advice, an offer to invest, nor an offer to provide advisory or investment management services.

It is also not my intention to state, indicate, or imply in any manner that current or past results are indicative of future results or expectations.

As with all investments, there are associated risks that can cause you to lose money. You alone are responsible for evaluating the benefits and risks associated with using an online broker and investing. You are also responsible for deciding which securities and strategies best suit your financial situation, goals and risk profile.

Prior to making any investment, you should consult with your own investment, accounting, legal and tax advisors to evaluate independently the risks, consequences, and suitability of that investment. Please speak with a professional that you know and trust before you buy or sell stocks.

Extras

Take a Shortcut

Each chapter represents a step towards becoming a stock investor. Please read it from cover to cover. You may discover something new, or a different point of view.

Nevertheless, to help you get what you need, please feel free to use a shortcut:

➤ If you already know the basics about stocks and the stock market, jump to Step 3.
➤ If you're researching stocks to buy, go to Step 4.
➤ If you need help in finding an online broker, skip to Step 7.
➤ If you already have a portfolio with an online broker and aren't sure what to do next, flip to Steps 6 and 9.

Use the Excel Workbook

Get the free companion Excel workbook at the Modern Wealth Media website. It's a helpful tool for planning, researching, and tracking your stocks. The workbook also includes many of the calculations discussed in the book.

Now that you know about it, what are you waiting for? Visit:

http://www.modernwealthmedia.com/workbooks

...and get your copy of the workbook now!

STEP 1: UNDERSTAND
THE BASICS

What is a Stock?

Folks forget that a stock is a type of contract. It entitles a buyer to "ownership interest" or "equity" in a company.

Stock buyers (e.g., "shareholders") used to receive a paper stock certificate as proof that they owned shares. Companies now keep track of shareholders electronically, and rarely give certificates.

A CORPORATION IS LIKE A PIE. WHEN YOU BUY SHARES, YOU ARE BUYING A "SLICE" OF THE PIE.

THE SLICE REPRESENTS YOUR SHARE. THE RECEIPT REPRESENTS YOUR "CERTIFICATE" OF PROOF THAT YOU OWN THE SHARE.

You purchase "shares" when you buy stock. The quantity you buy determines your ownership interest in a company.

For example, if a company has one million shares available for purchase in the stock market (e.g., one million "shares outstanding"), and if you buy 100 of those shares, you own...

$$100 / 1,000,000 = .01\%$$

...of the company.

You become the sole owner of the company if you buy all one million shares. It's just like a pie: when you buy all of the slices, you own the whole pie!

Why Do Companies Offer Shares of Stock?

No surprise here. A company's decision to offer stocks to the public comes down to money.

All companies start out as private companies. They operate in secret, and don't openly discuss their financials.

Private companies get funding from various sources. This includes friends, family, angel investors, and venture capitalists. Their funding helps pay for research, employee salaries, equipment, and more.

Funding can come one of in two forms: a loan (e.g., "debt") or a percentage of the company (e.g., "equity"). A "creditor" provides loans, and an "investor" provides money in exchange for equity (e.g., ownership interest).

Anybody can invest in a private company. However, a private company has less oversight than a "public" company does. This makes private companies "high risk" to investors.

As a result, private companies have regulatory filing requirements when they solicit money. But if the investor is "accredited", the company gets an exemption.

Anyone can invest in a private company. However, private companies are high risk. So private companies seek "accredited investors". Soliciting them for money requires less regulatory paperwork than soliciting everyday investors.

Private companies seek out accredited investors, not everyday investors. Not because of money (although having money helps), but because of regulations.

Accredited investors have a net worth of at least $1MM, made more than $200,000 each year for the previous two years, plus other characteristics defined by the Securities Act of 1933 and amended by the Dodd-Frank Act in 2010.

The Securities and Exchange Commission (SEC) believes an accredited investor is financially sophisticated. As a result, private companies do not have to register for SEC oversight when they accept money from accredited investors.

This all unfortunately keeps everyday investors from buying shares of hot private companies like Google before they go public.

Accredited investors can even sell to other accredited investors. Brokerages such as SecondMarket® are popular places to trade shares in private companies.

Unfortunately, the accredited investor "well" may run dry. What happens when their funding capabilities end, or when investors demand a greater pool of people with which to trade?

A private company can open its doors to all investors by working with an investment bank to complete an "initial public offering" (e.g., "IPO"). Anybody with money can buy or sell shares listed in a public stock market (minors need a custodian).

Folks also call the public offering process "equity financing". Companies receive cash (also known as "capital"). In exchange, investors get shares. These shares provide the investors with ownership interest (e.g., an "equity stake") in the company.

What Happens After a Company Goes Public?

Companies receive money <u>only</u> when investors buy shares the first time after a public offering. Companies do not receive any more money as the shares trade after the public offering.

Therefore, a company may decide to make additional offerings of shares to the public to raise more capital.

All companies have in their bylaws how many shares they can sell to the public. It is at the company's discretion whether to offer all of them in the initial public offering.

If a company offers all shares, they can only offer more after an overwhelming positive vote from their governing board. Since offering more can dilute the ownership interest of current shareholders, a positive board vote is hard to come by. As a result, a company must balance each public offering with their current and future capital needs.

Governing Boards

Organizationally, a company's CEO reports to and/or is a member of the company's governing board. A board is a team of voted or appointed members. Their business experience helps a company become and stay successful. The company's bylaws define the board's responsibilities.

A COMPANY'S BOARD GUIDES A BUSINESS ACCORDING TO BYLAWS. THEY HELP A COMPANY ACT IN THE BEST INTERESTS OF ITS CUSTOMERS AND INVESTORS.

The board tries to keep shareholders happy by providing them with a steady increase of the company's value (manifested by a growth in share price). A board can even fire the CEO if it's in the best interests of the company and shareholders.

Once public, a company must follow regulations that protect the everyday investor. No company enjoys filling out the often extensive regulatory paperwork—which is like a threading a needle while running a marathon.

Without these standards, investors could receive misleading information from companies. This affects an investor's decision to buy or sell shares.

Supply and Demand

A company only receives money – e.g., "capital" – the first time investors purchase shares after a public offering. The stock will continue to be bought and sold between investors like a ping-pong ball, without any additional cash going to the company.

A company only receives money after a public offering. As shares continue to trade, the company doesn't receive any more money.

Pricing an initial public stock offering is a huge responsibility. It's like setting the price for a Smartphone launch. If the demand turns out to be high, the company could have made more money with the launch. However, if the phone goes on sale after the launch, the first customers will feel foolish for buying it at a high price.

If an offering price is too low, a company will miss receiving as much money as possible from the sale. For example, if an offering were priced at $15 and subsequent demand drove the stock higher, the company still only received $15 per share.

On the flip side, if the price is too high, investors will feel as if the company made the offering just to make money. It may be true (and it often is). However, this may hurt the company's reputation with its customers and shareholders.

Unhappy shareholders will sell their shares. Selling may drive down the share price due to the laws of supply and demand:

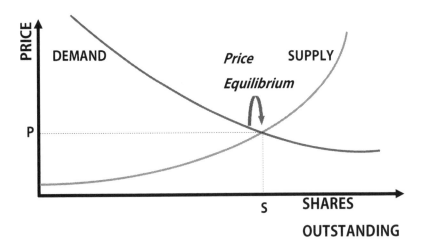

Unhappy shareholders will also lower the demand for a stock.

When demand decreases and the supply increases, the curves move left and right. The resulting price will be lower than the previous price.

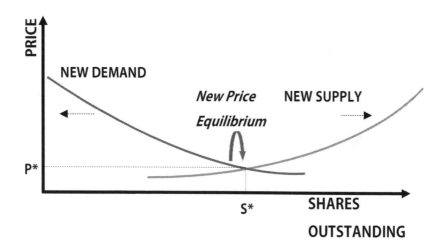

What a Falling Share Price Means to a Company

Although a company does not receive additional capital as shareholders trade stock after the IPO, the CEO and employees typically own a considerable amount of stock.

Therefore, the CEO and the governing board have an extra incentive to keep outside shareholders happy so that the stock price remains healthy. This keeps everyone's stock-based compensation healthy.

Also, a company may want raise money in the future with another stock offering. But they can't raise money if no one wants to buy their shares.

All of this means that you're not just a stockholder. You also have a seat at the table with the CEO. You voice your opinion on a company's business by buying or selling its stock.

As demand for a stock changes, its stock price can change for the better (or for the worse). This impacts the company's future prospects.

As a shareholder, you voice your opinion on a company by buying and selling its stock. As a shareholder, you have a seat at the board table.

Types of Stock

When you buy stock, you choose between common shares or preferred shares. I'm usually talking about common shares unless noted otherwise.

Common Shares

Preferred shares may sound preferable (no pun intended). Don't let the name mislead you. Common shares provide significant rights, including the right to:

✓ Receive dividends (e.g., a percentage of corporate earnings) if the company pays them to shareholders. The amount of money shareholders receive fluctuates.

✓ Enjoy a profit when you sell your shares at a higher price than your purchase price

✓ Vote on corporate governance matters (if the common stock shares provided by the company have voting rights)

Preferred Shares

The main differences between preferred and common stocks include:

➢ Lack of voting rights

➢ A fixed dividend

➢ Priority in getting one's money back if a company goes bankrupt

Preferred shares also have a steadier price than common shares. Retirees may appreciate this. However, expect less profit when you buy preferred instead of common shares.

Keep in mind you can convert preferred to common shares (but not vice versa).

How You Earn a Profit (and Lose Money) with Stocks

Imagine you bought 100 shares of Microsoft at $23 per share. This cost you:

$23 x 100 shares = $2300 to buy 100 shares of Microsoft (plus commissions, which is a fee charged by brokers).

In this example, your "cost basis" (e.g., your acquisition cost) is $2300 plus commissions.

Your cost basis is the original acquisition cost of your shares. Your cost basis determines the total amount of profit and loss you make when you sell your shares.

Profits

If your stock rises to $30 and you sold your shares, you would receive:

$30 x 100 shares = $3000 (less commissions) returned back to you if you sell after the price rises

You pocket the difference between what you bought the stock for and what you received back after you sold your stock:

$3000 - $2300 = $700 profit (less commissions)

Losses

If the stock falls to $20 and you sold your shares, you receive:

$20 x 100 shares = $2000 (less commissions) returned back to you if you sell after the price falls

You lose the difference between what you bought the stock for and what you received back after you sold your stock:

$2000 - $2300 = $300 loss (less commissions)

Buying more shares (and having a greater ownership interest) magnifies your profits and losses. If you bought double the shares in our example, your profit would also double:

($30 - $23) x *200* shares = $1400 profit (less commissions)

Owning more also magnifies your losses:

($20 - $23) x *200* shares = $600 loss (less commissions)

As a result, it's vital that you plan your stock purchases carefully and honestly assess whether you can withstand losing some or all of the money you invest.

Is Profit Free Money?

There's no such thing. There's always a catch, and in the case of buying stocks, it's taxes.

Capital Gains Taxes

If you sell at a profit *less than* a year after your buy, you pay "short-term capital gains taxes" on the profit you receive. Today's rate is the same as your ordinary income tax rate.

If you sell *more than* a year later, you pay "long-term capital gains taxes". Today's rate is 15% (or 0% if your tax bracket is 10% or 15%).

In the US, capital gains taxes has been a hot button in nearly every federal tax debate since the Revenue Act of 1921.

Presidents have not shied away from using the tax rate as a lever to affect economic activity (and support from contributors!).

For example, both President George W. Bush and President Barack Obama passed and extended a lower long-term capital gains tax rate in 2003 and 2008 respectively. Always research the latest rates before you buy or sell.

Loss Carryover

If you sell at a loss, you can receive a deduction on your taxes. Today, you can deduct up to $3000 in one year, and apply losses exceeding $3000 on future tax returns. It's a common strategy to sell losing stocks before the tax year ends (also known as "taking your losses").

Investors may use losses to offset capital gains taxes on profits. Although you have to pay taxes on your profits, you can offset your liability by deducting your losses.

Wash Sales

What's stopping a clever investor from selling a losing stock before the tax year ends, writing off the loss, and then buying the stock back? The wash sale.

If you sell then buy back your original stock or similar stock within 30 days, you cannot write off the loss. This is a "wash sale". Regulators add this old loss to your new stock's cost basis instead.

A WASH SALE HAS NOTHING TO DO WITH CARS. BECOME FAMILIAR WITH THEM, ESPECIALLY IF YOU ARE AN ACTIVE INVESTOR.

A higher cost basis means less profit or more loss when you sell. As a result, you will get the tax benefit of the old loss when you sell the new stock.

This may sound complicated. But you basically can't get sneaky with your buys and sells in order to rack up deductions on your taxes. Somebody already thought of that, so the IRS put a law in place to outlaw it.

Consult your own tax advisor concerning the application of federal and state tax laws to your particular situation.

What Benefits Come From Owning Stocks?

You may receive dividends as a shareholder.   A stock's "dividend yield" tells how much you may receive.

Dividends are "free" money (with "free" meaning taxable). Companies pay dividends with a check in a mail. Alternatively, they will directly deposit your dividends into your investment account if you set it up this way with your broker.

Companies share their earnings through dividends. The more shares you own, the more dividends you may receive.

You can use this money any way that you like – to buy more shares, or more shirts and shoes. The more shares you own, the more your proportional ownership.   And the more your proportional ownership, the more dividends you receive.

A company may pay dividends in stock shares too.   Nine times out of ten, however, a company will pay in cash.   Once again, you owe taxes on dividends you receive.

Common Share Dividends

Let's go back to the Microsoft example where you owned 100 shares. Assume Microsoft typically paid a 2% annual dividend. Also, assume Microsoft paid a dividend every three months (e.g, quarterly).

Even if Microsoft paid a 2% dividend in the past, they are not obligated to pay that much every year. The board announces the exact amount on the "date of declaration". The board will communicate that date to the public and media.

On the declaration date, a company will also give the "record" and "ex-dividend" dates.

In this example, Microsoft announces a $.125 per share dividend on the date of declaration. The board "records" on the record date that they owe shareholders $.125 per share.

In order to get dividends, you need to own shares by the company's "ex-dividend" date. It's typically 2 days prior to the record date. If you buy shares after the ex-dividend date, you will not be included in the next dividend payments.

Your dividend payment in this example would be:

$.125 per share x 100 shares = $12.50 quarterly dividend in your pocket

A company sends your dividend to you on the "payment date".

Preferred Share Dividends

If you owned preferred shares in this example, your dividend would be a fixed percentage of Microsoft's IPO price.

For example, if Microsoft's IPO price was $20 and if in its prospectus Microsoft agreed to pay preferred shareholders 7% annually, your annual dividend would always be:

7% x ($20 IPO price x 100 preferred shares owned) = $140 in dividends

Check a stock's prospectus for the exact terms.

COMPANIES CAN PAY YOU DIVIDENDS AS LONG AS YOU ARE A SHAREHOLDER. IT'S ONE OF THE KEY BENEFITS TO OWNING SHARES OF A COMPANY.

But not all stocks pay dividends!

The more established the company, the more likely they will pay a dividend to shareholders.

Mature companies (e.g., "blue chips") such as IBM and GE are not expecting their sales to grow year over year. As a result, the share price may not move very much.

This isn't a bad thing. Year after year, these companies may profit from a loyal customer base.

In other words, these companies have a significant share of their potential customer base already. They may earn more than enough income from their products and services to pay expenses. They usually don't need to reinvest their earnings to pay for research.

They can then afford to pay shareholders a sizeable chunk of their excess earnings via dividends.

Paying dividends also entices investors to buy their stock since a mature/blue chip company's stock price may move minimally.

As of the printing of this book, savings accounts pay low interest rates. More and more savers look to stable dividend-paying stocks like blue chips as an alternative.

Is a Stock a Bond?

Stocks and bonds are opposites. A stock provides ownership interest in a company. A stockholder enjoys profits and endures losses from being a part owner.

A bond, on the other hand, is an IOU or loan. When you buy a bond, you become a creditor to the company. You receive "interest payments". Ultimately, you get a bulk repayment from the company.

Investors buy bonds in the "debt market". Raising money with bonds is called "debt financing". Several types of entities can offer bonds to the public, including:

➤ Corporations (e.g., corporate bonds)

➤ Cities, states and other local governments (e.g., municipal bonds or "muni's")

➤ Countries (e.g., government bonds). The US, for example, sells Treasury bonds or "treasuries".

STOCKS AND BONDS ARE OPPOSITES. STOCKS MEAN OWNERSHIP. BONDS MEAN INDEBTEDNESS.

A Quick Primer on Bonds

You lend money to an entity when you buy a bond. You become a "bondholder", and the money that lend is called "principal".

If you ever took out a loan, a bank would typically act as your creditor. In the case of a bond, *you're* in the bank's position. *You're* the one lending money!

Without going into too much detail since this a book about buying stocks online, five characteristics you should know about bonds are:

➢ Maturity Date: The date that the company repays the bondholder. Interest payments to the bondholder stop.

➢ Face Value: The amount repaid to the bondholder when the bond "matures". This is also known as a bond's "par" value.

➢ Market Price: The bond's purchase price in the bond market. This can be more (e.g., "selling at a premium") or less (e.g., "selling at a discount") than the face value.

➢ Coupon Payments: The "interest" a bondholder can expect to receive while owning the bond. It's equivalent to a stock's dividend.

➢ Yield: The total profit a bondholder can expect to earn from buying and holding a bond until maturity. Yield includes profit earned from receiving coupon payments, and profit earned from buying a bond at a discount to its face value.

The profit you earn as a bondholder isn't free money. You owe taxes as you receive coupon payments. You also pay taxes on any profit at maturity.

However, you can receive "free money" by buying municipal bonds in the state where you live, or by buying a government bond. Both are "tax-exempt".

Both will give you tax-free coupon/interest income on the state and federal levels. If you buy a tax-exempt bond outside of your home state, you may pay state taxes.

This does not cover all of the tax consequences from owning and selling tax-exempt bonds, so please do your own research consult your own tax advisor concerning the application of federal and state tax laws to your particular situation.

Using Bonds to Raise Money

Established companies with a strong sales history can raise money by selling bonds to investors. It's similar to how individuals with a strong credit history can get better loans from banks.

Companies avoid giving away equity ownership by offering bonds to the public instead of stock. However, it's a negative to see a high amount of debt on a company's balance sheet since that debt has to be repaid (plus interest).

Too much debt can drag down growth. While companies may want to avoid giving away equity, they can't rely on raising money with bond debt.

Key Takeaways

✓ Stocks give shareholders "ownership interest" in a company proportional to the number of shares owned.

✓ "Ownership interest" lets shareholders receive a share of a company's earnings through dividends, and keep profits from selling stock.

✓ Companies provide stock to the public through an initial public offering ("IPO"). The company receives money only after the first purchase of their stock after a public offering. Companies do not get money as the stock continues to trade.

✓ Be aware of your tax burden for selling profitable shares (e.g., capital gains taxes), and your tax benefits for selling losing shares (e.g., loss write-offs and carryovers). Discuss the application of tax rules to your situation with an advisor.

Congratulations, you got through the basics! Hang in there – the next chapter provides the kind of information that separates the recreational investors from the experienced investors.

When you make it through the next chapter, you will know more than the vast majority of individuals trading stocks today. Really! So please keep reading.

STEP 2: UNDERSTAND HOW THE MARKET WORKS

The hardest thing investors have to control is the six inches of brain between your ears.

Even experienced investors have trouble staying calm sometimes. Knowing how the market works may help.

How is a Stock Price Determined?

Initial Public Offering Price

A company and its investment banking advisors set the IPO price. If they make it too high or low, somebody is going to look foolish.

To keep that from happening, the analysts from the bank exhaustively analyze financial statements to figure out the company's worth. They call this process "valuation". It's similar to appraising a house.

If analysts and investors are on the same page, then the company has got itself a reasonable IPO price.

ANALYSTS REVIEW FINANCIAL STATEMENTS IN ORDER TO VALUE A COMPANY AND DETERMINE AN APPROPRIATE INITIAL PUBLIC OFFERING PRICE.

A company's profits – or earnings – form the core part of the formula used to price an IPO. Analysts may also use future earnings expectations in their valuation.

This may happen with popular companies who aren't profitable before going public. An offering price can be set in hopes that the company will cash in on its popularity after the IPO.

IPO Fundraising Example

Let's consider a small advertising company that wants to offer investors 50,000 shares. Let's also assume the company's annual expenses are $945,000 and annual earnings are expected to be one million ($1MM).

The company decided to go public with an IPO price of $11 per share. Investors should expect a return on their investment (e.g., ROI) of:

($1MM-$945,000) / ($11 IPO price x 50,000 IPO shares) = 10% ROI to investors

In return, these investors provide the advertising company with:

$11 x 50,000 shares = $550,000 capital raised by the company

The company received $550,000 from its IPO. To get it, the company had to give up control of 50,000 shares to shareholders.

Daily Market Price

Once the IPO is complete, share prices will rise and fall based on supply and demand. If buyers want a stock, its price will go up. And vice versa – just like eBay or any market with a finite supply of goods.

These forces are also known as "free-market" forces. No governing body sets prices nor regulates supply and demand in the stock market.

Stock "Sale" Price

If a great stock appears to be "on sale", it is selling at a price that does not reflect its worth on paper (e.g., valuation). Investors searching for "value" will buy it.

It's the same feeling you get when you see an amazing house overlooking a beach for a price you can actually afford. You would buy it if you had the money because you'll feel like you're getting a deal.

Stocks can appear to be on sale.

When a stock trades at a "sale price", its market price may not yet reflect its

full potential.

Investors can perform their own valuation. They may realize the current and/or expected earnings are higher than what's reflected in (e.g., "priced into") the price of the stock.

An investor may then buy with the expectation that other investors will eventually realize the same thing. Once the secret is out, buyers may drive up the price due to demand.

WHEN DEMAND INCREASES, THE PRICE OF A STOCK MAY RISE. THE LUCKY INVESTOR BUYS THE STOCK BEFORE THIS HAPPENS!

Battling Other Market Participants

News Travels Fast!

Today's market is more "efficient" than ever. It's even nonsensical at times. News and whispers influence a stock's price faster than before. As a result, it's now much more difficult for investors to find undervalued stocks.

Believe it or not, reactions to news stories can have as much of an impact on stock prices as bad earnings or lousy products!

Sellers can drag down the price of any stock—even great stocks. This is why investors cannot be afraid to buy quality investments "on a dip" when the overall market declines.

An estate for sale on the beach may have to lower its price temporarily after a shark sighting. Similarly, great stocks can be dragged down for temporary reasons.

You're Not Alone in the Market

More than everyday individual investors participate in the market. You are joined by:

➤ Programs that trade electronically based upon news and other factors

➤ Institutional investors representing big corporate wallets that can trade large amounts of shares

➤ Pure technical traders who buy and sell repeatedly based solely on trends in a stock's price, and not on value

All of these participants can cause a stock's price to move for reasons besides a stock being a good or bad value.

As an investor looking for undervalued stocks, do not get caught up in trading a stock because you are see its price move.

Let me repeat – don't be fooled by price movements potentially caused by other market participants playing the sandbox who may not be reacting to value. That's an easy mistake made by new investors. Focus on the company's quality and value before you buy or sell.

WHEN YOU INVEST, YOU PLAY IN THE SAME SANDBOX AS MANY OTHER TYPES OF INVESTORS. WATCH OUT!

Some regulators argue these professional participants should be isolated from everyday, individual investors. That debate continues on today.

Do You Have to Use a Broker to Buy or Sell Stocks?

You don't. You just need to find someone willing to sell shares if you are a buyer, or buy shares if you are a seller.

Most of the time, you need help. In particular, to ensure all of the steps involved with transferring the shares happens to the letter of the law. This is where a broker becomes helpful.

A broker can be a firm or an individual licensed under the Financial Industry Regulation Authority (FINRA) to buy or sell investment products based on your order instructions.

When you want to buy or sell a stock with a broker, you start the process by placing an order. The broker executes your transaction for a fee called a "commission".

The commission can be a percentage of the amount of your order, a standard fee, or a hybrid (e.g., a percentage with a minimum fee).

You tell a broker in your order "what", "when", and "how much" you want to trade. A broker then executes your order on your behalf according to your instructions.

By the way, do not send your order instructions over email. Emails are not secure and can be hacked. You should give your instructions in person (ideal), over the phone, or – as we will see in the next section – online.

Where Does My Money Go When I Invest in Stocks?

When you place your order, your broker attempts to execute your order through one of four keys ways:

Route 1: To a market maker

A market maker – also known as a "dealer" or "principal" – is similar to a person running a shop on eBay.

This person or firm has a sizeable inventory of stock. They compete for orders from brokers by publicizing prices of shares from their inventory.

Since a market maker enables market participants to buy and sell when they need to, market makers are "liquidity providers".

They enable the smooth flow of buys and sell for a stock by buying from sellers and selling to buyers as needed.

Route 2: To a stock exchange floor broker

Exchanges like the NYSE still operate in the classic style seen in Wall Street movies. Traders meet face-to-face on the stock exchange floor to trade stock.

A floor broker will negotiate (e.g., "work") an order with a "specialist". A specialist is type of market maker who negotiates auction-style with brokers. Together, they complete orders from the specialist's inventory of stock.

Floor brokers and specialists primarily negotiate large orders from institutions. These orders can affect supply. Affecting supply can change the market price for a stock.

As a result, the floor broker and specialist will execute large orders using the specialist's private inventory. The public market supply will not get impacted this way.

When small orders (usually from everyday, individual investors) route to an exchange floor, floor brokers and specialists do not personally negotiate those orders. The order routes directly to a specialist's order book for execution instead.

Route 3: Via an electronic communications network (ECN)

An ECN connects buyers right to sellers, peer to peer.

In this case, your order executes when you connect with an investor who is selling if you're buying (and vice versa).

Certain exchanges like NASDAQ are fully electronic. They do not use floor brokers. They simply provide systems that connect buyers and sellers directly.

Route 4: To an internal inventory of stocks

Large brokerage firms like Citigroup Global Markets Inc. have the size and money to provide market maker services from their own account.

Brokers who provide this service are known as "dealers" or "principals".

A broker at a dealer firm can execute your order from an inventory of stocks held at his or her firm instead of routing the order elsewhere.

The process where a broker completes an order using his or her firm's internal inventory is called "internalization".

No surprise here – brokerage firms that provide both broker and dealer services are known as "broker/dealer" firms.

When a broker/dealer sells from their inventory at a higher price than the inventory's purchase price, the broker/dealer makes a profit.

Institutional investors prefer broker/dealers since dealers isolate these large trades from the open market supply. Otherwise, the institutions risk changing a stock's price while their order executes.

Best Execution

Brokers have a legal obligation to make sure that you get the best price for your order – e.g., "best execution".

This includes having infrastructure that can route your order to the best "liquidity" source quickly. Brokers also must execute your orders before executing orders for the same product in their own personal accounts.

In today's day and age, "best execution" is determined in a split second by the trading infrastructure at a brokerage firm.

BROKERS MUST ENSURE THAT YOUR ORDERS ROUTE THE SOURCE THAT PROVIDES YOU WITH THE BEST PRICE.

Is a Broker an Advisor?

No. The financial services industry regulates brokers and advisors differently. Brokers and advisors have different obligations in making suitable recommendations to clients.

For example, a broker may think it's suitable to feed child string beans for dinner. In particular, if the broker knows that string beans are generally beneficial to the child. The broker would know this after profiling the child in a process called "Know Your Customer".

On the other hand, an advisor may say that it's not in the child's best interest to have string beans if the child had string beans for breakfast and lunch.

The financial services industry regulates brokers and advisors differently. Brokers and advisors have different levels of accountability when making recommendations to clients.

It's such a subtle difference on paper. But it's a big deal in real life when two financial professionals can give different recommendations to the same person.

FINRA

The Financial Industry Regulatory Authority (also known as "FINRA") regulates and oversees *brokers* and brokerage firms.

The licenses FINRA requires a broker to have (including the Series 7) allow brokers to buy and sell securities on your behalf for a commission. These licenses do not discuss compensation for advice.

Brokers earn money when they buy and sell (which makes me envision – no offense – a shark, always in pursuit of the next transaction). While it is a tough way to make a living, it can also be very lucrative.

If a broker gives you a recommendation, they can only show you FINRA-approved sales material. Brokers have a legal obligation to provide you with broadly suitable recommendations.

Let's go back to our example. While string beans may benefit you, it's your responsibility to determine whether you should eat string beans again. It is not the broker's responsibility.

In short, brokers have a lower level of regulatory accountability for a client's overall best interests than an advisor.

The Investment Adviser's Act of 1940

This act regulates licensed *advisors*, who typically hold a Series 66 license. It requires the highest level of accountability to provide clients with advice that is in their best interests.

You may have also heard this referred to as "fiduciary responsibility" or "fiduciary standard".

The standard applies not only to advice, but to anything an advisor does that may impact the best interests of a client. This includes fully disclosing all conflicts of interest – in particular, with business dealings and compensation.

For example, an advisor *cannot* recommend to one client to buy a stock while being compensated for another transaction that may cause the price of that stock to fall. A broker, however, technically can.

KNOW WHETHER YOU ARE WORKING WITH A BROKER OR AN ADVISOR.

THE DIFFERENCE MAY MEAN WORKING WITH SOMEONE WHO MAY OR MAY NOT HAVE THE "FIDUCIARY RESPONSIBILITY" TO ACT IN YOUR BEST INTERESTS.

Discussing Compensation with Your Broker or Advisor

Do not get confused by terms used by advisors and brokers when you discuss compensation! Brokers work on commission. Advisors charge a fee. However, hybrid payment structures are starting to become popular.

➢ Commission: When a broker buys or sells on your behalf, they receive a "commission" – e.g., a percentage of the transaction.

➢ Fee-Only Advisors: Fee-only advisors do not charge a commission when they buy and sell stocks. They may charge an annual flat fee to manage your account. Or, they may bill you an annual percentage of your account's value.

➢ Fee-Based Advisors: A hybrid compensation structure that includes fee- and commission-based payments.

Advisors use a broker to route and complete client orders. However, fee-only advisors do not pass along the broker's commissions to their clients.

More and more advisors like myself are setting up their practices as fee-only. This removes the conflict of interest of being paid when an investment is bought or sold. Moreover, our compensation may increase as your account size increases. So our interests are aligned.

Brokers, Reps, and Advisors...Oh My!

Brokers and Advisors may be called many things – the names suitable for print follow below!

Brokerages or broker/dealer firms may refer to their brokers as "Stock Brokers", "Registered Representatives", "Stock Sales Representative", or simply "Reps". Brokers must have a Series 7 license to allow them to sell securities to non-institutional investors (e.g., "retail" investors).

Advisors typically work at Registered Investment Advisory firms, and may be referred to as "Investment Advisor Representatives", "Financial Advisors", "Investment Advisors", or "Financial Planners". An advisor must have a Series 66 license (which is a combination of the Series 63 and 65). These licenses allow advisors to provide advice for a fee.

An easy way to understand whether you are working an advisor or broker is to ask about compensation. Their answer may tell you more than trying to memorize what the licenses mean.

Certifications

You have seen it before – e.g., the alphabet soup behind the name of an advisor or broker: CFP, CFA, ChFC and more.

I have mixed feelings about certifications. Certain certifications – in particular, the CFA for portfolio analysts – provide spectacular training experience. When you see ones like this, you know the professional didn't just pass a test and sign a check to get it.

I have unfortunately seen brokers and advisors with other certifications which did not – in my opinion – separate them from the pack in terms of experience and skill.

A general rule of thumb that I advise is if you're considering working with an advisor or broker who doesn't have more than ten prior years of Wall Street/financial services experience, he or she should have a certification.

Why ten years? Over that timeframe, a professional in this industry would have likely seen both up and down markets. They should have the experience (and battle scars) to provide knowledgeable advice going forward.

Regardless of experience or certifications, always understand how your money is being invested. Never continue a relationship with a professional who doesn't clearly explain his or her recommendations. In other words, if you have an uncomfortable feeling in your gut, move on.

Your gut can be your best guide when you invest.

Speaking of uncomfortable feelings...

Be cautious with brokers and advisors who recommend products (usually mutual funds) created by their own firms. The professional may not have the incentive to tell you about the best product if recommending their firm's product provides his or her firm with additional compensation.

An "independent" firm does not have that conflict of interest.

Also, be wary of the phrase "I've got a hot investment for you". Peddling one investment at a time screams salesperson, not advisor.

A broker or advisor should present an investment to you as part of a discussion of your goals. They should also clarify how the investment will help you reach your goal.

What Are My Options Besides Using a Live Broker?

Once again, you are not legally required to use a live broker or advisor when you buy and sell shares. Two common alternatives exist for individual investors to circumvent working with a broker or advisor:

Direct Investment/Direct Stock Plans

Investors can buy stock directly from certain companies that offer "direct stock plans". Companies advertise these plans on their websites.

You may be able to get stock at a lower price via a direct stock plan. This depends on how the plan calculates its stock prices (which can be found in the plan's disclosure documents).

These plans may allow you to purchase stock commission-free. You may have to pay an administrative or other fee to participate in the plan.

The bad news is you usually have to be an employee of the company in order to participate in the plan.

When you buy stock in a direct stock plan, your account can *only* contain stock for the company offering the plan. This can cause a portfolio management hassle for you if you participate in plans at multiple places. It is surprisingly easy to lose track of these types of accounts.

While you may be able to use software to see a unified overview of multiple accounts, you lose the ability to transfer money between investments. You will also have to keep track of multiple versions of plan rules.

As a result, participate in a direct stock plan only if you're getting a great deal on the price, and only if you can keep track of your account. Otherwise, another alternative exists, which is why I wrote this book.

Discount Brokers

FINRA still classifies "discount brokers" as "brokers". In this case, a company – not a live broker – executes your order.

Investors buy and sell via a discount broker without the benefit of receiving recommendations from a live, licensed broker. Live advice comes at a premium.

Discount brokers charge cheaper commissions because they aren't providing clients with the live broker experience.

Instead, clients use do-it-yourself research and management tools to find investments and manage their portfolios.

Investors like not having to use a live broker. However, the do-it-yourself aspect has shot many people in the foot.

Managing a portfolio of stocks by yourself will never be easy, and it's not for everyone. However, by the end of this book, the process will hopefully be less mysterious, and the way forward more clear.

Stay encouraged, keep putting one foot in front of the other, and keep reading!

The Genesis of Discount Brokers

Placing Orders in the Old Days

Investors used to call or telegram a broker to place an order. It sure seems like a long time ago. However, individuals typically bought stocks this way up until the late 90's.

The Digital Age changed this process.

More people had internet access. Performing transactions online become more commonplace and familiar.

Individuals soon began to look around and ask what else could they buy online.

Investors, in particular, began to ask for ways to manage their own accounts without having to go through a live broker.

To capitalize on the growing desire to buy stocks online, brokerage firms gave online accounts to existing clients. These accounts had lower to no commissions.

At this point, however, the majority of people trading online were experienced investors. They already owned stocks, and had past experience working with a live broker.

These investors would even get a step-by-step walkthrough of how to buy stocks online with their live broker on the phone!

That bit of history is often forgotten – e.g., the guidance that early online investors had, and their prior experience. Also, nearly every stock rose in the 90's, which made do-it-yourself investing less intimidating.

As a result, the idea of using a discount broker became an approachable concept, and a new industry took flight.

IT WAS EASY FOR AN INVESTOR TO PICK A STOCK AND PROFIT IN THE 1990'S WHEN NEARLY EVERY STOCK ROSE IN PRICE. THIS MADE DO-IT-YOURSELF INVESTING MORE APPROACHABLE AND POPULAR.

The Emergence of Discount Brokerage Firms…and Pain

A class of full-blown discount brokerages like E-Trade exploded in popularity in the late 90's.

Investors traded 100% online without the benefit of having a relationship with a live broker. An investor simply placed an order, and the discount broker's primary responsibility was best execution. As a result, commissions were cheaper.

Business boomed for discount brokerages. More investors wanted to take the reins of their portfolios. Many dreamed of becoming the next internet millionaire. Trading volume grew as more individuals participated in the market.

The 2008 financial crisis made
  thousands of online investors realize
            that they never really learned how
to research stocks and how to
                    manage their portfolios.

People believed they could sign up with an online broker, and do as well as a professional investor. But if you had a tray of medical instruments, would you operate on yourself? Given a law book, would you defend yourself in court?

Inevitably when the market crashed in 2008, online investors who never truly learned how to invest experienced a great deal of pain.

Traders vs. Investors

I've mentioned the words "trading" and "investing" in nearly every paragraph so far. Do you know the difference between the two?

If the universe of stocks represented children, investors would represent a parent. Investors provide the resources for stocks to grow stronger. They hope that the stock uses its wisdom and experience to grow over the long term.

Traders, on the other hand, represent an aunt or uncle. They will visit when the stock is having a good day. However, once the stock starts to lose steam, a trader may take the first exit stage left!

INVESTORS WILL NURTURE A STOCK, ENCOURAGING IT TO GROW AND PROVIDE GREAT PRODUCTS OR SERVICES TO THE WORLD.

Investors have more concern for the overall business growth, earnings, cash flow, and other internal "fundamental" factors of a business. Generally, an investor stays invested over a longer time horizon – e.g., 3-5 years or more.

Traders act on short-term opportunities, and are more interested in quick profits. Traders look for price momentum signals, trends and other external "technical" signals. Once the trend ends, traders may exit their position.

Certain types of businesses like hedge funds and electronic trading engines operate as a combination of both, making short and long-term plays.

It helps to know before you start buying stocks whether you want to be an investor or be a trader. In this book, we're focusing on investing (although I love aunts and uncles too!).

Without a Live Broker's Help, How Do You Know Which Stock to Buy? And When to Sell?

By using the same techniques that they use, modified for everyday investors.

I know...I've made you suffer long enough. You made it through enough information to make you more knowledgeable than an overwhelming majority of individual investors trading online today. So kudos and congratulations!! Keep on reading.

Key Takeaways

✓ A great stock could be dragged down temporarily due to news or a trading event that increased the supply of shares outstanding. Do not be afraid to buy a quality stock when the price takes a dip.

✓ Brokers and advisors have different levels of responsibility when making recommendations. Know whether you are working with a broker or an advisor by asking about compensation. Brokers are typically paid commissions, and advisors a fee.

✓ The first non-professional online investors had prior experience. They benefited from having an educational relationship with a live broker, and traded during the 1990's when nearly every stock rose in price.

✓ While discount brokers provide convenience and cost savings, lack of education hurt new investors trading for themselves during recent recessions.

Before We Continue…

I urge you to download the free companion Excel workbook so that you can work while you read. You can get it at the Modern Wealth Media website:

http://www.modernwealthmedia.com/workbooks

How to Claim Your Copy of the "Stocks Online" Workbook:

➢ Visit **http://www.modernwealthmedia.com/workbooks**
➢ Download the workbook
➢ Subscribe for future updates

Throughout the book, I added a note like the one below to guide you to the right place in the workbook so that you can work along while you read:

WORKBOOK GUIDE: GO TO THE "MY BUDGET" TAB.

STEP 3: ANSWER THESE THREE QUESTIONS

Forgive me for sounding like every advisor working today, but perhaps you can relate to this analogy:

Would you jump into your car and go on a cross-country drive without a map?

It's true, right? Why would you exit your front door unless you had a purpose and destination? In other words, why would you get in your car and spend money on gas unless you had a plan for your journey?

Even if you plan to ride around in your car and sing along to your favorite tracks in private, and drive back home, you have a purpose and a destination!

LIKE ANYONE TAKING A JOURNEY, SUCCESSFUL INVESTORS NEED A PURPOSE AND A DESTINATION.

Having a plan ensures that you will get to your destination without wasting time or money! Investing successfully requires the same purposeful mindset.

So before you jump in and buy shares of a stock, make sure you know the answer to the next three questions.

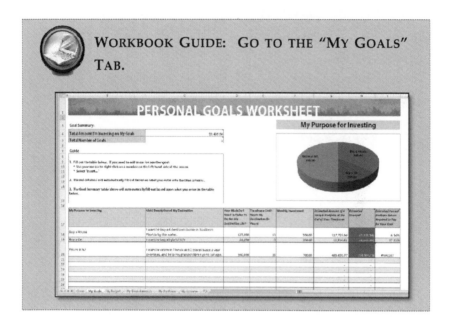

Question 1: Why Are You Thinking About Investing?

When companies started to replace pension plans with self-directed 401K plans in the 1980's, investing became a part of everyone's vocabulary. Everyone had to invest in his or her own account in order to save for retirement.

As a result, the number one reason why individuals think about investing is to save for retirement.

Nevertheless, you may have a short-term goal. Perhaps you would like to buy a home in 5 years. Or, perhaps you are saving for your child's college education.

Think about every reason why you would want to invest. Use the next sections as a guide in articulating and documenting your reasons.

Define Your Purpose for Investing

To help, I included the top 10 reasons clients have come to me for investment advice:

1. To save for retirement
2. To save for a home
3. To save for college
4. To supplement my income
5. To reduce taxes on savings (for example, with municipal bonds)
6. To take advantage of a bull market (which is a rising market)
7. To get a higher return than a savings account
8. To invest on behalf of a child (e.g., custodial account)
9. To save for a new business
10. To invest in a particular stock or sector

Whatever your reason or reasons, write down a one-sentence summary of each reason and proceed to the next paragraph.

 WORKBOOK GUIDE: UNDER "MY PURPOSE FOR INVESTING", ENTER A BRIEF SUMMARY OF EACH OF YOUR GOALS. THREE SAMPLE GOALS ARE INCLUDED.

Vividly Describe Your Destination Lifestyle

First, select one of your purposes. Let's use retirement as an example. Close your eyes and envision the day when you start using the savings you built up by investing.

Which city are you living in? Are you living in an apartment in the city, or a house in the suburbs? Do you have a garden? A wine collection? How often do you eat out and travel? What do you do for a hobby?

You can visualize every type of purpose – even one where you're just supplementing your income. In that case, how many days per week are you working? What type of work are you doing? What do you do every day when you are working less and living off your investment income?

Take the time to create as vivid a picture as possible. If it helps, sketch your thoughts on a paper, or clip pictures or articles from a magazine. Paste it on poster and create a vision board—I did!

Do whatever you need to build up your vocabulary for describing your destination.

Once you have your description for each purpose, write it down, and proceed to the next paragraph.

 WORKBOOK GUIDE: UNDER "VIVID DESCRIPTION OF MY DESTINATION", ENTER A DETAILED DESCRIPTION OF A DAY IN THE LIFE OF EACH PURPOSE.

IMAGINE A DAY IN THE LIFE OF EACH GOAL. THIS HELPS MAKE THEM MORE TANGIBLE. IT'LL THEN BE EASIER TO BUILD YOUR PORTFOLIOS.

Estimate the Cost of Your Destination Life

Come back down to Earth for a moment.

You just designed a destination for each purpose. Creating vivid pictures will help you estimate how much your destination costs.

Think about those destinations. How much money do you need in today's dollars to pay for your destination life?

For example, if your destination is "to be rich", well…what is "rich"? When do you know that you are rich? What does rich look like?

If you are at least able to say, "I want a billionaire's life with a private jet and estates on every coast", that helps! I just hope that helping others is also part of the picture!

Now, determine – in today's dollars and excluding taxes – how much money you would need on a monthly basis if you lived the destination that you envisioned today. Multiply that number times 12 to get an annual estimate, and write down your estimate for each goal.

If it helps, estimate the monthly cost of *each part* of your destination picture (e.g., the jet, the estates, the wine collections, etc.), add the estimates together, and then multiply by 12 to get your annual estimate.

It is very important not to change your destination picture yet, even if you know that it will cost a surprising amount of money to succeed.

Get your initial estimate on paper first for each destination. As you continue to determine what you need to save, you can figure out what adjustments you need to make so that you can achieve your goals.

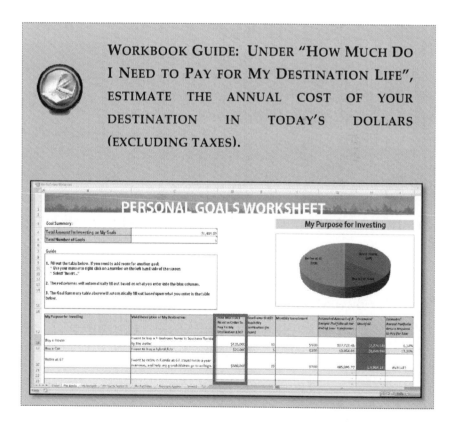

WORKBOOK GUIDE: UNDER "HOW MUCH DO I NEED TO PAY FOR MY DESTINATION LIFE", ESTIMATE THE ANNUAL COST OF YOUR DESTINATION IN TODAY'S DOLLARS (EXCLUDING TAXES).

REMEMBER YOUR ESTIMATE SHOULD BE IN TODAY'S DOLLARS, AND PRE-TAX. PLEASE DISCUSS THE IMPACT OF TAXES ON YOUR SAVINGS WITH AN ADVISOR.

Why Advisors Treat Retirement Planning as a Special Case

One of your goals may be to retire with a particular lifestyle.

Retirement goals differ from other goals like buying a home. Planning for retirement has many more inputs that determine your future cost of living.

For example, during the 20-30 years of retirement, Washington may change tax rates and may alter Social Security and Medicare rules. You may also go from being self-sufficient to needing to long-term care. Unexpected expenses may also arise – in particular, medical expenses.

Retirement also is a type of goal where once you hit the destination, you will still need to keep a portion of your savings invested so they will grow above inflation. In other words, you must continue to invest so that your savings do not lose "purchasing power". A stamp won't stay 45 cents forever.

For simplicity in this book, I am assuming a one-time bulk payout at the end of your timeframe. Also, assume that the amount that you are targeting to save for retirement in the workbook only includes your after-tax savings.

Please keep in mind that for "ongoing" goals like retirement, your investment plans may have to continue past the point when your destination life begins. Also, stocks are just a part of the solution. Insurance, bonds, and other types of products are typically part of a retirement plan as well.

As a result, please talk with a financial professional that you trust to solidify your investment plans for more complex scenarios.

Question 2: What is Your Timeframe?

When you take a car trip with your family to the Grand Canyon, you plan the vacation to start and end within a specific timeframe.

Otherwise, you may end up driving around for longer than expected. You could also spend more money than expected. In addition, if you are taking vacation from a job, you might lose your job!

By when do you want to retire? Or, in an ideal world, how many years from now would you like to buy your home?

For each purpose, write down your ideal timeframe in years before you start living that destination life.

 WORKBOOK GUIDE: UNDER "TIMEFRAME UNTIL I REACH MY DESTINATION", ENTER A TIMEFRAME FOR EACH PURPOSE IN YEARS.

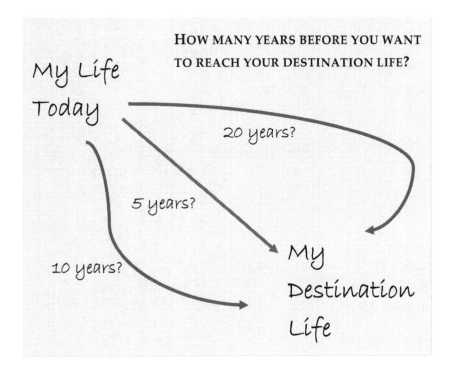

The Luxury of Time in the Market

There is no greater friend to investing in stocks than time in the market for two reasons:

Reason 1: Time to Recover From a Decline

Even quality stocks can decline due to unrelated negative news or a poor economy.

Time in the market gives your portfolio time to recover. Even one bad summer can take almost a year for your portfolio to snap back.

For example, the market declined over 13% in less than 3 weeks during the summer of 2011 (July 22 – August 10).

Investors watched as Standard and Poors downgraded the US and economic uncertainty brewed in the Eurozone:

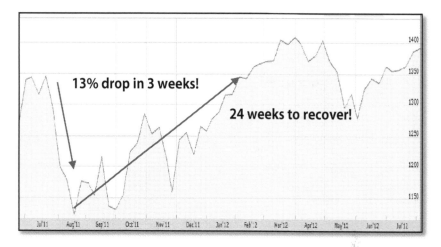

The US market had a strong recovery, but took until Feb 24, 2012, for the market to get back where it was 6 months prior!

The market even double dipped downward on October 3, 2011 before it recovered.

If you had a portfolio in the stock market on July 22, 2011, you needed to wait until March 2012 to become profitable again.

I'm sure you are thinking that on July 22, 2011, you would have cashed out and got back in on either August 10 or October 3. However, I'm warning you now that getting back into a market after just getting out takes nerves of steel. Nevertheless, I will teach you techniques that may help.

Having the luxury of time in the market allows you to take a longer view. As a result, you may not have anxiety over what may be a temporary drop.

This example shows that as you get towards the end of your timeframe, it may make sense to get out of the stock market. More about this too in an upcoming chapter.

Reason 2: Compounding

Stock investors enjoy benefits from owning dividend-paying stocks. If an investor reinvests cash from dividends – e.g., uses the cash to buy more shares – he or she would enjoy the benefit of owning more shares that *also* grow *and* pay dividends!

Your portfolio's value "compounds" when you set up your dividends to pay dividends. Its overall value accelerates.

Don't forget you have to be an existing shareholder in order to receive dividends. If you try to time being in and out of the market, you may miss being a shareowner on the stock's record date (which is the date when a company's board allocates dividends to shareholders).

Compounding also occurs as your portfolio grows. If you invest $5000 into a stock that grows 10% after your first year, your portfolio value would be:

$5000 + ($5000 x 10%) = $5000 + $500 growth = $5500 after your first year.

What if the stock grows another 10% by the end of the second year? Your portfolio will *not* grow by just $500 again.

Remember, the value of your portfolio at the beginning of your second year was $5500. As a result, 10% of growth will make your portfolio's new value be:

$$\$5500 + (\$5500 \times 10\%) = \$5500 + \$550 \text{ growth} = \$6050 \, !$$

Think of compounding like a growing a plant. In your plant's first year of growth, it may only grow two stems. However, in your plant's second year of growth, each stem may also grow two stems. And at the end of your plant's third year of growth, each stem grows another two stems. And so on.

Your plant does not grow just two stems each year. Instead, the number of stems multiplies each year. The more time you allow your plant to grow, the more growth upon growth your plant will have.

By the Way...What is the S&P 500? How does it help investors?

The S&P 500 measures the overall health of the US economy. It's made of 500 stocks, picked and maintained by Standard and Poor's (a ratings agency) since the early 1900's.

Each stock represents the performance of an industry in the US. Collectively, the stocks reflect the overall state of the US economy, using Standard and Poor's methodology.

Other companies publish indices. For example, Dow Jones publishes the Dow Jones Industrial Average (e.g., "The Dow") which tracks the performance of 30 US blue chip stocks.

In fact, countries around the world publish indices to help track and communicate the health of their economies.

These indices not only help investors quickly understand how an economy's health changed over time. Indices also help investors compare their portfolios to a market that best matches the kinds of stocks they own.

Portfolio managers call this comparison process "benchmarking".

If you know how your portfolio stacks up against a "benchmark" like the S&P 500, you can quickly discern your portfolio's performance by watching the index.

We will discuss how to use a benchmark to keep on top of your portfolio's performance in Step 5 of this book.

WORKBOOK GUIDE: DON'T FORGET – UNDER "TIMEFRAME UNTIL I REACH MY DESTINATION", PUT THE NUMBER OF YEARS BEFORE YOU WANT TO ACHIEVE YOUR DESTINATION LIFE.

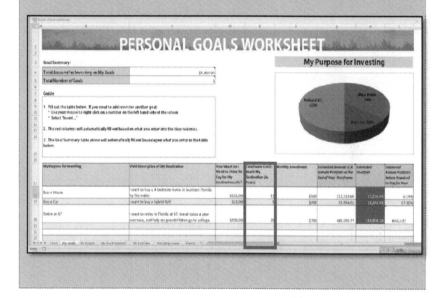

Question 3: How Much Are You Willing to Invest (and How Often)?

Questions 1 and 2 helped you determine:

- ✓ Your purpose for investing and your ideal destination life
- ✓ How long before you want to reach your destination life

We are finally at the step where you take the steering wheel of your life. You will determine what action you need to take today to guide your life towards the destination you want.

You will not only figure out how much you can invest, but also how much you *need* to invest to achieve your goals.

> *Anything worthwhile is worth* *fighting for. Only you will* *fight for the life you desire.*

Whatever you do, do not get discouraged in this step. Do not put the book down and give up. Anything worth having is worth fighting for.

Right now, you're fighting for the future self you want to become. Only you will fight hard for you. So do not give up on yourself.

You will thank yourself for taking what feels like painfully meticulous steps to plan your life. I promise you that if you are stressed out today, you will feel a tremendous amount of relief once you develop a clear roadmap for yourself.

Put Investing Into Your Monthly Budget

Your budget should not only have the usual monthly expenses (e.g., groceries, utilities, entertainment, and more), but also line items where you are "paying yourself".

Paying yourself includes not only saving a portion of your income into a savings account (including emergency savings), but also investing for your future.

100% of your income should be "working". Make it work by either paying for expenses, or paying *you* back towards your goals.

If you don't track your income, extra money will go to an extra pair of shoes. There's nothing wrong with treating yourself. Nevertheless, you do not want to be eighty-five with an awesome shoe collection from forty years ago!

By consistently watching your budget, you'll get yourself back on track if you see that you're spending recklessly.

I would argue that unless you have a clear picture of you current cash flow situation, you could not possibly start investing. Otherwise, you risk putting too much of your savings into the stock market. Or not enough.

So get out your bills from last month, and figure out today where your money goes each month.

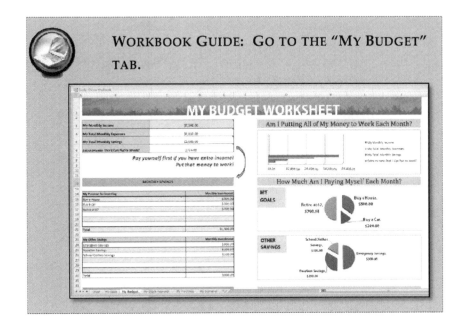

On the workbook:

☐ Put how much money you receive as income (after taxes) on a monthly basis by "My Monthly Income" at the top of the workbook.

☐ Write each purpose under "My Purpose for Investing". Then, estimate how much you *think* you can save for each goal on a monthly basis. Note that if retirement is a goal, only include the money that you're saving out of your take-home pay. This does not include money saved in your employer-sponsored plan or pension.

☐ Write in other savings into the "My Other Savings" table.

☐ Finally, write in your monthly expenses into each of the tables below "Monthly Expenses".

The workbook will calculate:

✓   Your Total Monthly Expenses
✓   Your Total Monthly Savings
✓   Extra Income that you Can Put to Work!

If you have extra income, consider adding more to your emergency savings, or to your investment goals. Keep in mind that 4-6 months of emergency savings is advisable – however, speak to an advisor you know and trust to determine the right amount of emergency savings for your situation.

If your expenses exceed your savings, the "Extra Income That I Can Put to Work" will turn red:

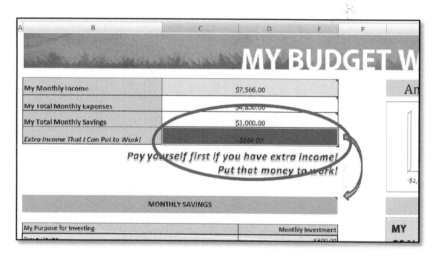

Consider how you can lower your expenses. If you cannot lower your expenses, you may need to save less under "Monthly Savings".

Once you completed your Budget worksheet, <u>return to the "My Goals" tab</u>. Write your **monthly investment** amounts from the "My Purpose for Investing" table on the "My Budget" tab into the "Monthly Investment" column on the "My Goals" tab.

Why Invest Each Month?

Congratulations for completing your budget! You can check off something most people never do in their lifetime.

Rarely do I advise putting all of your savings into the stock market at one time. If you are lucky, the market will continue to rise after you invest.

However, if you do not have a lucky Leprechaun in your corner, the market may fall again before rising. You'll lose money before earning it back.

Why risk putting *all* of your savings into the market if Murphy's Law says you'll lose before you make money?

As a result, if you're starting your investment journey with a significant amount of cash savings, spread your savings over 6-12 months and invest a portion at a time. Once that time period passes, continue to invest what your budget allows each month.

By investing each month, you will buy shares at different prices. You avoid buying a bunch of shares at the wrong time. This method even has a name: "Dollar Cost Averaging".

Think of dollar cost averaging as nibbling into an unknown fruit. Would you pop the whole fruit into your mouth, or would you take little bites as a precaution?

While dollar cost averaging does not guarantee that you will not lose money, it will help put less of your total savings at risk at one time.

To help keep up the discipline of investing each month, I recommend setting up an electronic transfer from your bank account into your investment account, and arranging a standing order to invest your deposit into a portfolio of stocks.

But first, talk with an advisor to determine what is suitable for your situation.

Determine If You Are Saving Enough for Your Goals

Now that you have a comprehensive budget, you know how much of your savings you *think* you want to invest monthly into each goal. But is it enough?

Financial planners estimate how much a portfolio may grow over time – including contributions – so they can advise clients on whether they need to invest more today.

The workbook will really come in handy for this step. First, ensure you entered how much you think you can save on a monthly basis into the "Monthly Investment" column on the "My Goals" tab. The workbook will estimate how much a hypothetical portfolio that grows 6% per year will grow to by the end of your timeframe.

The workbook will also estimate by how much you may miss your target under the "Estimated Shortfall" column. Finally, it'll calculate how much you need your portfolio to grow annually in order to pay for your destination life:

As you can see for my "Buy a Home" purpose, I have a shortfall!

I need to either buy a cheaper house, invest over a longer timeframe, save more, or invest in a more aggressive portfolio.

By the Way...A Message About Diversification

If someone asked you to walk off the edge of a building holding a balloon, would you ask for one big balloon or a bunch of smaller balloons?

If you're not sure, ask yourself what would happen if a bird hit your balloons. Your one big balloon would pop, while perhaps just a couple of your smaller balloons may get affected.

Diversification in a portfolio helps to reduce the risk of being exposed to one "factor" – e.g., one country, one industry, one company, and so on.

Diversification does not guarantee that you will not lose money. However, it may improve your chances of keeping your money if one part of your portfolio has trouble.

If you do not have enough money to create a portfolio with 5-10 different stocks, you may not have enough diversification. In this case, other products may be more suitable (for example, mutual funds).

Nevertheless, you can still step into the stock market with quality stock investments.

As always, invest at your own risk.

What if You're Not Saving Enough?

If you are able to save toward each of your goals, you've successfully fought half the battle!

What if it's looking like you're not able to save enough to get the destination life that you want? You may have to tweak some things.

This may be upsetting. But if your timeframe and the amount of money that you're able to invest today won't get you to the destination life that you want tomorrow, take hold of the wheel and take action now. Below are four ways to fix a shortfall:

➢ Tweak Your Destination Lifestyle: Instead of a 4-bedroom home in Florida, perhaps you can retire in a less expensive 3-bedroom home.

   Revisit the description of your destination life, and attempt to pare down its cost.

➢ Extend Your Timeframe: Instead of buying a car in 5 years, check if you can save more if you bought a car in 7 years.

   Take advantage of time in the market as well as time to invest in order to increase how much you ultimately save.

➢ Reduce Your Expenses: Here's where having your monthly expenses organized in a budget helps. Look at where the majority of your money goes each month, and try to make some adjustments.

Perhaps you brew your own coffee at home in the morning. Or, get cash back on your purchases through programs like Ebates. Stop subscribing to magazine you don't read (that's a common cost-cutter). Cancel your gym membership, and buy a jump rope. Over time, little cutbacks make a big difference.

➤ Increase Your Income: This exercise may be the spark you need in order to push towards having a better career today.

You don't have to give up on your dream. Successful people fight for their dreams. Since you already made it this far into this book, you too are successful. Now…continue fighting and make adjustments!

Portfolio Return

The amount your portfolio grows or shrinks each year is called your portfolio's return. In exchange for investing your money, what did your portfolio give back to you? What did it "return" for your investment efforts?

Advisors build portfolios with a desired "average annual portfolio return" in mind.

Why average? Unlike a money market or savings account, your stock portfolio will not grow by the same amount each year. Some years, your portfolio will do very well, and some years it may not.

As a result, an advisor will use an average as a target. Over the long term, all of the years of ups and downs in your portfolio should average out the target value. If your actual average return starts to veer off target, an advisor will adjust the stocks in your portfolio.

Why is Knowing Your Desired Portfolio Return Important?

If you're putting together a basketball team, you wouldn't put together a team filled with all Lebron James-type players. Or all Kobe Bryant's. You would want a Dwayne Wade, a James Harden, and a Carmelo Anthony to round out your team.

In other words, each stock in your portfolio has a role, and each brings its own "return" that collectively contributes to your overall portfolio return.

For example, if you have all Blake Griffin-type players – who is an aggressive, high flying player – you may win certain games by a big margin. That style of play, however, will not win every game.

Therefore, as coach you would not risk having a team of just aggressive, high-flying players. You may balance out Blake Griffin's style with other styles (e.g., passers and defenders).

If you pick the right team of quality yet complimentary players, you as the coach would increase the likelihood of winning more games.

If you pick the right portfolio of quality yet complimentary stocks, you will increase the likelihood that you'll have a consistent return each year. If you're able to consistently make the return you need, you will ultimately achieve the ability to pay for your destination life.

As with basketball players (and I won't name names), past performance can be used to *estimate* future performance, but past performance is not a *guarantee* of future performance.

CONSISTENTLY AIMING FOR AN AVERAGE ANNUAL PORTFOLIO RETURN MAY HELP YOU ACHIEVE THE ABILITY TO PAY FOR YOUR DESTINATION LIFE WITH YOUR INVESTMENTS.

Should I Pay Off My Debt First Before Investing?

The problem with debt – in particular, credit card debt – is the dreaded interest payment. The longer you have credit card debt, the more interest you pay.

Ideally, you want your savings to go towards the thing that gets you the best return.

If you invest in the stock market, your savings may only grow at a rate of 6-8% in an average year. However, if you pay off your credit card, you're effectively getting a 25% annual return since you're paying less interest.

In this day and age, however, it may take 10 years or more to pay off a credit card. So the question becomes should you forgo time in the market in order to pay down your debt?

Instead of forgoing time in the market, balance your credit card payments with your investment savings.

You ultimately need to pay off more than the card balance grows each month. To figure this out, add together:

➤ How much interest your credit card company charges you in a month, plus...
➤ Your minimum required payment, plus...
➤ How much you spend on the card each month (ideally, you *aren't* spending on a card with a balance).

Your monthly card payment should be more than that total. Not less than, and not equal to. If you are not paying more, you will never pay down your card and should not be investing.

Ideally, you would pay off your debt before you started investing. However, you do not want to hold your future hostage to spending mistakes of the past. Just keep the mistakes in your past, and keep saving and investing to get the future you desire.

Putting it All Together

At this point, you know:

✓ Your purpose for investing
✓ Your desired destination
✓ Your timeframe
✓ How much you can invest on a monthly basis

You now have a basic financial plan that incorporates several of your goals! That is a BIG DEAL, so congratulations!!

In the next chapter, we will begin the process of selecting stocks that may help you reach each of your goals.

Are you ready? We are just getting started with the meat of the book! I'm enjoying taking this journey with you.

Key Takeaways

✓ The first step in investing includes understanding why you are investing (e.g., your purpose), and what your end goal looks like (e.g., your destination).

✓ Next, determine how many years you have until you want to reach each goal (e.g., your timeframe).

✓ Finally, put how much money you'll dedicate to saving and investing in your budget. Determine if you are investing enough by estimating how much a hypothetical portfolio would grow.

✓ If you have a shortfall, don't hesitate tweaking your destination goal, extending your timeframe, cutting your current expenses, or increasing your income in order to save more towards your goals. Only you will fight for the life you want.

An Advanced Look at Risk

If you are driving and see a yellow light, are you the type who would punch the accelerator, or slow down?

This may give you insight into whether or not you are a risk taker.

Investing involves the risk of losing your money. Unlike a savings account, you can lose money if your stock falls to lower price than what you bought it.

Let's look at a $5000 investment placed in a savings account in 1998 that earns 2% annually. Compare it to a $5000 investment in a stock in 1998. The stock mirrors the S&P 500 index:

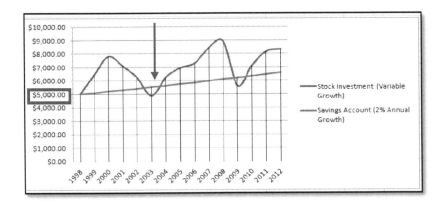

Notice in 2003, the curvy line for the stock investment falls below $5000 (e.g., $4855.11). But by 2008, the stock almost doubled its original value!

An investment in the stock market has more risk than a savings account. Investors take this risk to enjoy a bigger profit if they chose stocks wisely.

Unfortunately, bigger profits require bigger risk. Investors wanted to control this risk. Eventually, a whole area of portfolio management developed over the years to examine and manage these risks.

Analysts started analyzing stocks' "risk characteristics". They call this "portfolio analytics" or "quantitative strategies".

Like a baseball player, each stock has statistics that tell you whether it may be risky, including:

➢ Historical Beta/Beta Coefficient: This tells an investor the sensitivity (e.g., volatility) of a stock in comparison to a related benchmark (for example, the S&P 500).

For example, a stock with a beta of 1.5 will in theory move 15% higher if its benchmark increases 10%, or 15% lower if its benchmark falls 10%.

A technology stock like Baidu.com has a beta of 1.84 today, whereas a blue chip stock like Proctor and Gamble has a beta of .44.

If relevant benchmarks rose 10%, Baidu.com would in theory increase 18.4%. Proctor and Gamble would increase only 4.4%.

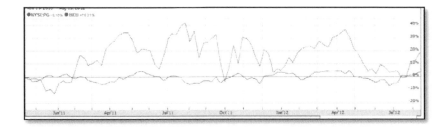

The top line shows Baidu.com's returns over the past two years. The bottom show's Proctor and Gamble's returns.

You may see that a higher beta usually means higher and lower price swings. This causes greater volatility in the value of your portfolio. And ultimately, greater risk of losing your principal.

➢ Standard Deviation: Standard deviation also measures a stock's volatility – however, it is in comparison to the stock's mean/average return.

A high standard deviation means a stock's actual return may fluctuate in a wide range around its average annual return. In other words, the return that you get may differ almost wildly year-to-year.

A stock like Baidu.com has a higher standard deviation than a stock like Proctor and Gamble. Year-to-year, Proctor and Gamble's return has stayed close to its mean value. Baidu.com has had up and down years where its return varied significantly.

Not many advisors and authors talk about portfolio risk. However, it is one of my favorite areas of finance. I truly enjoy educating my clients about it.

As a result, analyzing risk and calculating a target portfolio return are definitely part of the strategies in this book.

STEP 4: FIND STOCKS THAT SUPPORT YOUR PLAN

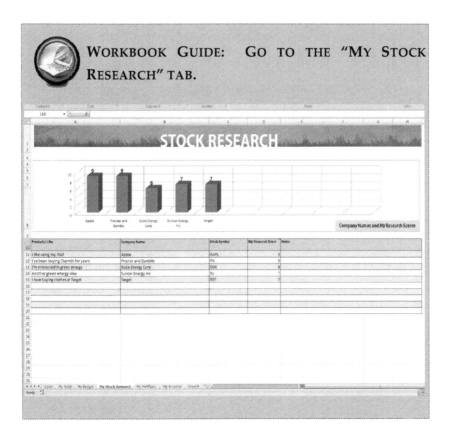

If all of the stocks in the world could apply for a position in your portfolio, you would receive over 65,000 resumes! It would take a ridiculous amount of money and time to manage that many stocks.

Learn how to whittle down this universe of 65,000 stocks into a shortlist. Pick ones that support your plan by providing you with the annual return you need. Also, find ones that have at the right level of risk.

It's a dirty job, but someone has to do it.

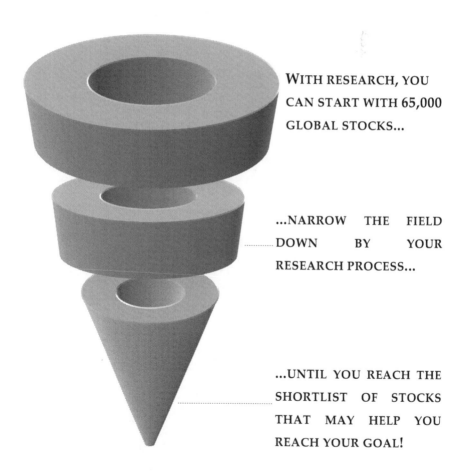

WITH RESEARCH, YOU CAN START WITH 65,000 GLOBAL STOCKS...

...NARROW THE FIELD DOWN BY YOUR RESEARCH PROCESS...

...UNTIL YOU REACH THE SHORTLIST OF STOCKS THAT MAY HELP YOU REACH YOUR GOAL!

Draft a List of Ideas

Finding great investments isn't rocket science. If you love a company's products, then you already know if it can attract customers. And a successful company needs – at minimum – loyal customers.

Look around at the things you love, and consider investing in those companies.

For example, can't live without your iPad? Add Apple to your list of ideas. Do you always buy Viva paper towels? Write down Johnson and Johnson.

By drafting your list of ideas this way, you will benefit from already knowing what financial analysts spend hours researching – e.g., does this company have a loyal audience that will provide increasing revenue over the long term?

If you love a company's products, *you already know that information.*

Perhaps you also feel strongly about the future of a "sector". For instance, if everyone you know takes prescription medicine, perhaps you feel strongly that Health Care or Biotech will have increasing sales over the long term. So add those sectors to your list.

As you become more used to finding investments this way, ideas will jump out at you. You'll naturally think like an investor.

If you don't know which company creates the product that you love, go to http://finance.google.com. Type your product's name into their search field, and click the blue search button. Google will return the name and stock symbol of the company!

This technique underpins the golden rule of investing: first, buy what you know.

Subsequently, as you become a successful stock picker using this strategy, your radar will notice other investment ideas using the same technique.

As you get used to creating a shortlist of stock ideas from your day-to-day observations, your radar for finding investment opportunities will become sharper.

WORKBOOK GUIDE: GO TO THE "MY STOCK RESEARCH" TAB. WRITE A BRIEF DESCRIPTION FOR EACH PRODUCT THAT YOU LIKE IN THE COLUMN "PRODUCTS I LIKE". WRITE IN THE NAME OF THE COMPANY THAT CREATES THE PRODUCT IN THE "COMPANY NAME" COLUMN.

USING GOOGLE FINANCE, LOOKUP THE TWO- TO FOUR-CHARACTER STOCK SYMBOL:

➢ IN A BROWSER, GO TO HTTP://FINANCE.GOOGLE.COM
➢ IN THE SEARCH FIELD AT THE TOP, TYPE A COMPANY NAME
➢ THE STOCK SYMBOL IS AT THE LEFT OF THE NAME OF YOUR COMPANY (FOR EXAMPLE, "COST" FOR COSTCO).
➢ WRITE THIS SYMBOL IN THE STOCK SYMBOL COLUMN IN THE WORKBOOK.

10-Step Stock Research Process

Now that you have a list of ideas, dive in to research your ideas!

In this step, we are checking whether your ideas make great investment opportunities. And by great, I mean does your idea have the potential to grow and provide you with a nice profit and/or dividend.

A great investment idea should also help you create a portfolio that will meet your goal.

As you become the master investor that I know that you will become, you'll develop your own research technique that reflects your personal point of view and even your personality.

While you take that journey to developing your own investment technique, please feel free to leverage the research roadmap below. It's one that I've personally used to find value investments for clients and for my own portfolio:

10-Step Stock Research Process

1. Understand the Company's Business
2. Check the Price, and Evaluate the Price and Volume History
3. Check Style Fundamentals
4. Evaluate Sector and Industry Performance
5. Check Analyst Price Targets and Recent Headlines
6. Evaluate Market Share/Performance Relative to Competitors
7. Review Management Team, and Management Effectiveness
8. Check Institutional Ownership
9. Analyze the Financials
10. Analyze Technical Signals for Entry and Exit Points

As you evaluate a company, give it 1 point if you feel your stock idea passes a step.

I've found that stocks which scored 8 or higher have the quality and value to add to a portfolio. Stocks scoring between 6-8 went onto a watch list. Finally, I put stocks with a score of 5 or below to the side to reevaluate in a year.

It's Like Mining for Gold!

You may have noticed that most of these steps are common sense. In fact, value investors from Benjamin Graham to Warren Buffet have used similar steps to evaluate investments. If it ain't broke, don't fix it!

Nevertheless, each investor adds his or her own color to any process. I'll describe exactly what I'm looking for, step-by-step while using free online research tools. This will help you get inside of a professional's head to see this process in action.

You're mining the market for gold, so roll up your sleeves!

Free Online Resources

When you go online, you'll find an abundance of resources available to perform free, basic stock research. Almost too many resources!

The source that works best for you will depend on your experience. Sites that I have used in the past include:

> - ➢ Kiplinger's: http://www.kiplinger.com/investing
> - ➢ Bloomberg: http://www.bloomberg.com
> - ➢ Morningstar: http://www.morningstar.com
> - ➢ Yahoo! Finance: http://finance.yahoo.com
> - ➢ Google Finance: http://finance.google.com
> - ➢ Zack's Investment Research: http://www.zacks.com
> - ➢ Financial Visualizations: http://www.finviz.com
> - ➢ Stock Charts: http://www.stockcharts.com

Ones showing opinions from other readers can potentially show you misleading information. If anyone can post, then anyone can encourage buying or selling a stock. This could manipulate the price.

As a result, I encourage you to stick with sites that provide professional analyst recommendations.

Personally, I began using Yahoo! Finance for basic stock research over 10 years ago. I feel it's comprehensive and high quality. Google Finance also has an outstanding suite of free online research tools – including links to other solid industry sites. So for demonstration purposes, I'll use Yahoo! and Google in this book's examples.

About Paid Tools

As an advisor, I also use paid tools – for example, Morningstar's Advisor Workstation, SunGard, and a neural networks-based package for modeling called NeuroXL. However, when you're starting out, paying for research tools may be overkill.

10-Step Research Example

Let's put the 10-step process to work.

At the start of the year and at midterm in college, my friends and I would trek to Target to buy all kinds of school supplies. We could buy everything from comforters to tablets in one trip.

Target has grown up with me, becoming my source for foundational items at decent prices. Sometimes, I'm shocked at how low the prices are – really. I'm also a big online shopper, and look for the online-only deals.

I sound like a paid spokesperson, but I'm just a longtime fan of Target's.

But is Target a great stock?

My analysis follows, using the 10-step process plus free online resources. I recommend that you follow along at your computer with Target at first, and then research on your own with a stock from your shortlist.

Ready? Let's go!!

MANY PEOPLE, INCLUDING MYSELF, LOVE TARGET. HOWEVER, DOES THIS MAKE TARGET'S STOCK A GREAT INVESTMENT?

Note: I researched Target on July 29, 2012. Factors about this company may have changed since this book was printed. If you are considering Target, please complete a new evaluation with the latest news and stock information.

The evaluation below is not a recommendation to buy or sell Target. Invest at your own risk, and based upon your own objectives.

Before investing, it is highly recommended that you seek the advice of a professional.

Note that use of Google Finance, Yahoo! Finance, or any other site mentioned in the book, does not imply an endorsement by those companies for this book. I do not own shares of Google or Yahoo!. I am not compensated in any way for mentioning their names in this book.

Step 1: Understand the Company's Business

How to Setup Your Browser for This Step:

☐ Go to *http://finance.google.com*
☐ Type "Target" in the search field at the top of the page. Google will then show you recommended search results in a pop down field:

☐ Select "Target Corporation" from the pop down field. You'll arrive at the Google Finance homepage for Target.
☐ Scroll to the middle of the page to the "Description" section:

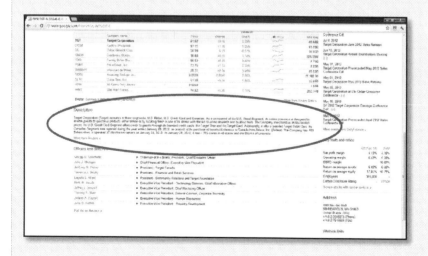

I've spent my fair share of afternoons cruising Target aisles for deals. This helped me understand already how Target makes money.

Nevertheless, it's a good idea to check how Target describes its business because the scope of it could be more than what customers see. So from Google Finance:

```
Description:

Target Corporation (Target) operates in three
segments: U.S. Retail, U.S. Credit Card and
Canadian. As a component of the U.S. Retail
Segment, its online presence is designed to
enable guests to purchase products either
online or by locating them in one of its stores
with the aid of online research and location
tools. The Company merchandise at discounted
prices. Its U.S. Credit Card Segment offers
credit to guests through its branded credit
cards, the Target Visa and the Target Card.
Additionally, it offer a branded Target Debit
Card. Its Canadian Segment was reported during
the year ended January 28, 2012, as a result of
its purchase of leasehold interests in Canada
from Zellers, Inc. (Zellers). The Company has
189 Zellers sites. It operated 37 distribution
centers at January 28, 2012. At January 28,
2012, it had 1,763 stores in 49 states and the
District of Columbia.
```

The "More from Reuters" link below the Description gives the complete description, where you can see that Target:

✓ Has been around since 1902
✓ Facilitates shopping in its brick and mortar stores on its website
✓ Has a credit card business, and business interests in Canada
✓ Owns several brands
✓ Can be a one-stop shop for all kinds of household essentials

No surprises here. Target's business centers on being a US retailer. Plus, its credit card and recent Zeller's acquisition appear to supplement and not contradict its core retail business.

In fact, after visiting Zeller's site, it appears to be an acquisition with the intent of spreading Target's core brand of "providing quality household essentials" into Canada.

Target appears to have passed this step. After each step, I'll summarize up my evaluation and provide a score using a scorecard like the one below:

	PASSED?	SCORE
Step 1: Understand the Company's Business		
Step 2: Check the Price, and Evaluate the Price and Volume History		
Step 3: Check Style Fundamentals		
Step 4: Evaluate Sector and Industry Performance		
Step 5: Check Analyst Price Targets and Recent Headlines		
Step 6: Evaluate Market Share and Performance Relative to Competitors		
Step 7: Review Management Team and Management Effectiveness		
Step 8: Check Institutional Ownership		
Step 9: Analyze the Financials		
Step 10: Analyze the Technical Signals for Entry and Exit Points		
TOTAL		

Step 1 Conclusion:

Target has been around for a long time. It appears to have a growing retail business that makes sense.

Scorecard:

	PASSED?	SCORE
Step 1: Understand the Company's Business	✔	1
Step 2: Check the Price, and Evaluate the Price and Volume History		
Step 3: Check Style Fundamentals		
Step 4: Evaluate Sector and Industry Performance		
Step 5: Check Analyst Price Targets and Recent Headlines		
Step 6: Evaluate Market Share and Performance Relative to Competitors		
Step 7: Review Management Team and Management Effectiveness		
Step 8: Check Institutional Ownership		
Step 9: Analyze the Financials		
Step 10: Analyze the Technical Signals for Entry and Exit Points		
TOTAL		

Step 2: Check the Price, and Evaluate the Price and Volume History

How to Setup Your Browser for This Step:

➤ Return to the Google Finance Target homepage (e.g., go to *http://finance.google.com* and search for "Target").

➤ At the top of Target's Google Finance homepage, zero in on the following three areas:

      1. "Last Close Price"

      2. "52-Week High and Low"

      3. The chart area

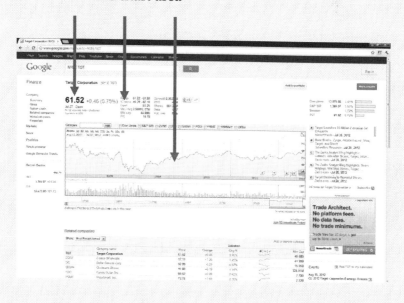

➤ On the chart, click "5y" in the upper left hand corner of the chart area near the word "Zoom" to see Target's price movement over the previous 5 years.

Note: At the top of Google's homepage for Target, you may see "(NYSE: TGT)". This means Target trades on the New York Stock Exchange (NYSE) under the symbol "TGT".

Google shows that Target had a close price (e.g., Target's market price when the NYSE market closed on July 27th at 4:30 pm EST) of "$61.52".

It's a decent price – an investor could pick up almost 50 shares over the course of a year with $250/month (depending on changes in the share price and commissions).

Looking at Target's 52-week high and low, its price ranged between $45.28 and $62.18 over the previous year. Comparing this range to Target's last close price, you can see that Target is trading at its highest price in over a year.

While this may make investors think the stock is on a roll, passing a 52-week high point holds psychological significance for traders.

This makes me question if the price will continue to rise, or if traders will get nervous and force down the price by selling and taking their profits.

Looking at the 5-year chart, Target's price has been steadily rising since the end of the 2008 financial crisis. This provided shareholders with consistently increasing share value.

Granted, Target did not increase its price by very much over the past 5 years. Nevertheless, at least the share value over time increased, and did not decline or stay the same.

Step 2 Conclusion:

Target has a decent market price and an encouraging price history. The timing does not appear to be ideal since its price just rose to its highest level in a year.

Nevertheless, the positives outweigh the negatives for this step.

Scorecard:

	PASSED?	SCORE
Step 1: Understand the Company's Business	✔	**1**
Step 2: Check the Price, and Evaluate the Price and Volume History	✔	**1**
Step 3: Check Style Fundamentals		
Step 4: Evaluate Sector and Industry Performance		
Step 5: Check Analyst Price Targets and Recent Headlines		
Step 6: Evaluate Market Share and Performance Relative to Competitors		
Step 7: Review Management Team and Management Effectiveness		
Step 8: Check Institutional Ownership		
Step 9: Analyze the Financials		
Step 10: Analyze the Technical Signals for Entry and Exit Points		
TOTAL		

Step 3: Check Style Fundamentals

<u>How to Setup Your Browser for This Step:</u>

> Return to Google Finance's home page for Target.
> Zero in on the statistics at the top of the page – in particular:
>
>   1. Mkt Cap
>   2. Div/yield
>   3. Beta

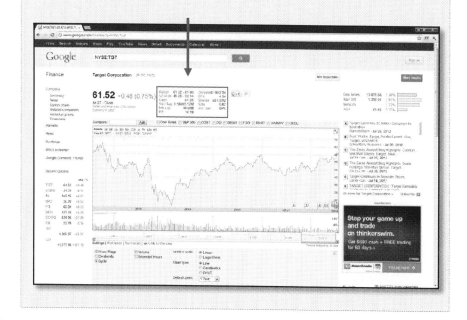

From the previous step, we already know that Target's price has had a steady rise over a moderate range since 2008. Should investors expect the same from Target going forward?

The following three statistics may help give you a feel for how Target's price may move in the future.

Market Capitalization

Target has a $41B market capitalization ("market cap"). That's the total value of all Target's shares in the stock market. At $41B, Target trades with the characteristics of a "Large Cap" stock.

The larger the market capitalization, the less volatile the stock usually is. Expect moderate changes in the stock's price, and few wide swings from day to day.

For reference, the ranges used for classifying companies by market cap are (going from largest to smallest):

➢ Mega cap: $200B+
➢ Large cap: $10-200B
➢ Mid cap: $2-10B
➢ Small cap: $250M-2B
➢ Micro cap: $50-250M
➢ Nano cap: Under $50M

Blue chip companies like Proctor and Gamble and Coke fall in the large cap or higher range. Younger, riskier companies typically fall in the small cap range and below.

Dividend Yield

Next, "Div/yield" tells investors a company's past dividend amount. A company may continue to pay dividends, but isn't obligated. Generally the higher the dividend yield, the less volatile the stock price.

Conservative, mature companies tend to pay dividends. Their earnings may pay for their expenses with some money left over. These companies may pay these excess earnings to shareholders via dividends to entice investors to buy and hold their stock. Popular blue chip companies have a dividend yield of around 3.5% or higher.

Target's dividend yield is 2.37%. It's more than the dividend at a growing company (approximately 1%), but less than what I like my conservative stocks to pay.

If the price of a stock moves moderately, I believe investors should receive a nice fat dividend. This will help keep the invested money from losing purchasing power due to inflation.

Although the inflation rate has been down since the 2008 financial crisis, the financial services community still uses 3-4% as a long-term guideline.

Target has had a solid year this year. So far in 2012, Target's price is up by 18%! Nevertheless, I'm cautious about whether I'll see growth like this in the future given Target's market capitalization and dividend yield.

Beta

Target's beta is .87. Beta tells investors the sensitivity of a stock's price in comparison a relevant benchmark (like the S&P 500).

A beta of .87 means if the benchmark moves up or down by 10%, Target's stock price will move up or down by 8.7%. That is less movement – e.g., less volatility – than the benchmark.

Note that since Target's beta is positive, its stock price tends to move in the same direction as the overall market – e.g., not down when the market moves up and vice versa.

<u>Step 3 Conclusion</u>

Target's appears to be a conservative stock. It had a great year so far in 2012, but I question how much its price will rise in the future. Its dividends are good, but I'd prefer a higher yield.

<u>Scorecard:</u>

	PASSED?	SCORE
Step 1: Understand the Company' s Business	✔	1
Step 2: Check the Price, and Evaluate the Price and Volume History	✔	1
Step 3: Check Style Fundamentals	✗	0
Step 4: Evaluate Sector and Industry Performance		
Step 5: Check Analyst Price Targets and Recent Headlines		
Step 6: Evaluate Market Share and Performance Relative to Competitors		
Step 7: Review Management Team and Management Effectiveness		
Step 8: Check Institutional Ownership		
Step 9: Analyze the Financials		
Step 10: Analyze the Technical Signals for Entry and Exit Points		
TOTAL		

Step 4: Evaluate Sector and Industry Performance

How to Setup Your Browser for This Step:

➤ Go to Target's Google Finance homepage.

➤ Scroll to the middle of the page. Target's sector and industry can be found right above the Description:

| ABAX: Financials | WMT | Wal-Mart Stores | 74.52 | +0.85 | 1. |

Sector: Services > Industry: Retail (Specialty)

Description

Target Corporation (Target) operates in three segments: U.S. Retail, U.S. Credit Card and Canadian. As a component of the U.S. R enable guests to purchase products either online or by locating them in one of its stores with the aid of online research and locator

A stock could be a great investment, but investors will move with caution if the stock's industry and sector are struggling.

Moving with caution doesn't rule out buying a great investment if it'll rise above the troubles of its industry and sector.

"Industry" and "Sector" are synonymous to a city and state – it is where a stock "lives" within the overall market. Checking up on these is like when you are searching for a place to live. You would scope out the neighborhood first to determine whether you would want to live there.

BEFORE LIVING IN A CITY OR STATE, YOU RESEARCH IT. THE SAME MINDSET APPLIES TO RESEARCHING AN INDUSTRY OR SECTOR BEFORE BUYING A STOCK.

Sector

In Your Browser...

➢ Click on "Services" (which is Target's Sector). Google will subsequently show a page with a chart at the top.
➢ Click on "5y" in the upper left hand corner of the chart.

You should now see a chart showing the "Services" sector performed compared to the overall market:

The graphs show that Target's sector and the overall market have had similar performance (e.g., "tracked") over the past 5 years.

Target appears to be in a fairly stable, reliable sector. Using the city/state analogy, wouldn't living in a stable "state" be desirable? Yes!

Industry

In Your Browser...

➢ On Target's Google Finance homepage, click on "Retail (Specialty)" (which is Target's Industry). Google will subsequently show a page with a chart at the top.
➢ Click on "5y" in the upper left hand corner of the chart, near the word "Zoom".

Target's industry ("Retail (Specialty)") has performed strongly in comparison to the overall market over the previous 5 years.

The top line shows how Target's industry performed, and bottom line shows the overall market's performance.

I'm taken aback by the two dips in the industry's chart. But overall, "Retail (Specialty)" grew more than the overall market the past 5 years.

Since an industry has a closer relationship to a stock's performance than its sector, seeing Target's industry outperform the market is encouraging.

Step 4 Conclusion:

Both Target's industry and sector performance show promise compared to the overall market.

Scorecard:

	PASSED?	SCORE
Step 1: Understand the Company' s Business	✔	1
Step 2: Check the Price, and Evaluate the Price and Volume History	✔	1
Step 3: Check Style Fundamentals	✗	0
Step 4: Evaluate Sector and Industry Performance	✔	1
Step 5: Check Analyst Price Targets and Recent Headlines		
Step 6: Evaluate Market Share and Performance Relative to Competitors		
Step 7: Review Management Team and Management Effectiveness		
Step 8: Check Institutional Ownership		
Step 9: Analyze the Financials		
Step 10: Analyze the Technical Signals for Entry and Exit Points		
TOTAL		

Step 5: Check Analyst Price Targets and Recent Headlines

How to Setup Your Browser for This Step:

➤ Return to the Google Finance homepage for Target
➤ Scroll down to the bottom of the page until you reach the "External Links" section in the lower right hand corner of the site:

➤ Click on "Analyst Estimates". A new tab or window will open on the MarketWatch site. MarketWatch provides news and opinions, as well as research data:

➤ Scroll down the page until you reach the "Analysts Recommendations" section.

At this point in our research process, you may think researching a stock is a detailed and arduous process! Major banks actually employ teams of stock analysts to do it.

An analyst may follow a sector (e.g., Utilities analysts, Technology analysts, etc.). Alternatively, an analyst may track a specific stock if its size or popularity warrants coverage.

Analyst opinions are *valuable.*

However, only use them as a reference and not a buy or sell trigger.

Banks may give analyst reports to clients, or to the public for a fee. To drum up publicity, a bank may release parts of a report for free, such as the Buy/Sell recommendation or price targets.

The full report of a stock may be useful to purchase if you're planning to invest a significant amount of money into a stock. You may also be interested in reading an analyst's thought process while researching a stock.

Sector or industry-level analyst reports may help you understand an area of the market that piques your interest.

But on an ongoing basis, the information such as what you're currently viewing on the MarketWatch site may be sufficient.

Keep in mind that while these opinions come from professionals, they should only be used as a reference and not as the sole basis of your decision to buy or sell a stock.

Analysts Ratings Explained

Under the "Snapshot" section, you should see list of juicy tidbits from analysts that you can use in your research:

Right off the bat, you can see that 26 analysts on average recommended an "overweight" action for this stock in investors' portfolios. What does "overweight" mean?

By my last count, there are at least 14 different ratings an analyst can give for a stock. Why?

"Buy" and "Sell" ratings used to be the industry norm. However, analysts began using less direct ratings like "Overweight" and "Underperform" to avoid appearing to manipulate the market.

The industry became sensitive to this after the late 90's, when certain superstar analysts could sneeze and get people to buy or sell a stock!

Here is a sampling of the various ratings that can be assigned to a stock by an analyst:

➢ Strong Buy: Highest buy recommendation.
➢ Buy/Overweight/Outperform/Accumulate: All   are   buy recommendations
➢ Neutral/Market Perform/Equal Weight/Hold: Don't buy but don't sell.
➢ Sell/Underweight/Underperform/Liquidate/Reduce: All are sell recommendations
➢ Strong Sell: Most severe sell recommendation (and rarely used)

Analysts can also provide estimates of a stock's future earnings and future market price.

As you are looking at these statistics, remember than analysts' ratings can vary wildly from analyst to analyst.

Looking an average recommendation of 10 or more analysts, or looking at trends may be the best way to digest these recommendations.

In Target's case, analysts estimated increased earnings for the current year versus last year. They also projected a target price very close to Target's current price. Looking at the bar chart, fewer analysts gave a buy rating and more gave this stock a hold rating versus 1-3 months ago:

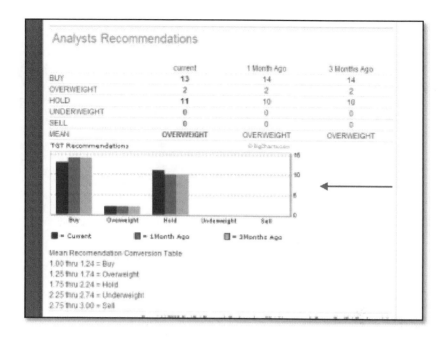

In conclusion, it appears that while analysts like this stock, the stock's "Buy" momentum with analysts may be losing steam.

It's a good idea to check the opinions on least one other site. It can't hurt to take a broad survey of analysts.

Yahoo! Finance has a great section with analyst estimates. Let's look there on the next page.

How to Setup Your Browser to See Yahoo! Finance Analysts' Estimates:

➢ Go to *http://finance.yahoo.com*
➢ Enter "Target" or "TGT" into the search field under the "Home" tab:

➢ After you click on the name in the search field drop down, you will see the Yahoo! Finance homepage for Target.
➢ Look at the menu on the left hand side, and scroll down until you reach the "Analyst Coverage" section.

After clicking on "Analyst Opinion" and reviewing their recommendations, I came to the same conclusion as I did from looking at the estimates on MarketWatch. Nevertheless, it's a good idea to double check this on multiple sites.

Back on the Google Finance homepage for Target, you can see recent news stories on the upper right hand side. Clicking on "All News for Target Corporation" will show an expanded view like this:

I'm primarily looking for trends in Target's news. Have they been reporting positive news recently – for example, for rising dividends, new products, or better than expected earnings?

I primarily see good news: news about expansion plans, a favorable story from a major bank about Target's sales trends, and more.

Click the "More on Reuters" link under the "Description" paragraph back on Target's Google Finance homepage, and go to the "Key Developments" tab at the Reuter's site. You'll see that on June 13th that Target announced an increase to their quarterly dividends. That's good news!

Step 5 Conclusion

The news and the analyst opinions appear favorable, although I have some concerns over whether Target's price may be losing steam.

Scorecard:

	PASSED?	SCORE
Step 1: Understand the Company's Business	✔	1
Step 2: Check the Price, and Evaluate the Price and Volume History	✔	1
Step 3: Check Style Fundamentals	✘	0
Step 4: Evaluate Sector and Industry Performance	✔	1
Step 5: Check Analyst Price Targets and Recent Headlines	✔	1
Step 6: Evaluate Market Share and Performance Relative to Competitors		
Step 7: Review Management Team and Management Effectiveness		
Step 8: Check Institutional Ownership		
Step 9: Analyze the Financials		
Step 10: Analyze the Technical Signals for Entry and Exit Points		
TOTAL		

Step 6: Evaluate Market Share/Performance Relative to Competitors

How to Setup Your Browser for This Step:

➢ Return to the Google Finance homepage for Target

➢ Zero in on the P/E value at the top of the page:

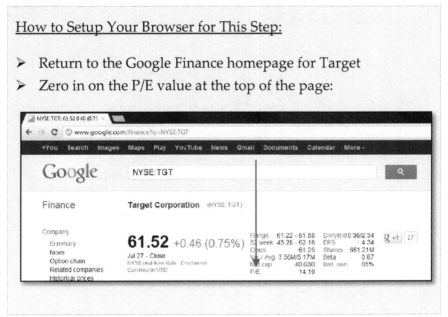

Target appears to be scoring well in our 10-step research process. Nevertheless, could a competitor be an even better investment opportunity? Is Target the best opportunity in its industry?

The quickest way in my opinion to compare two companies within the same industry is with Price to Earnings (P/E). It's the market price per share, divided by a company's annual earnings per share.

Price to Earnings tells investors how much the overall market desires a stock. The higher the P/E ratio, the more investors are willing to pay per dollar of earnings.

Certain industries have lower or higher average P/E. For example, most technology stocks have a higher P/E than utility companies. This makes sense because investors usually want to pay more for ownership interest in a technology company versus a utility company.

Don't use P/E as a standalone value. It only makes sense when you compare it to another company's P/E in the same industry, to an industry average.

The higher the P/E relative to other companies in its industry, the more the market already appreciates and values the company's earnings. Also, a relatively high P/E reflects the optimism that investors have expressed about a company's future.

If you're looking for undiscovered value investments, a relatively high P/E may mean the cat's out of the bag. Investors may already know about the stock and drove up the price.

A Low P/E Isn't Always an Undiscovered Value Investment

Here's where we hit a snag with Target.

Imagine being part of a panel of judges in a singing competition. You have the opportunity to sign one of two undiscovered singers. Only age differentiates the singers – one is 21 and the other 51.

The judges will likely have more optimism for the younger singer versus the older singer. Why? Because questions may come up about why the older singer isn't appreciated at this point in his or her career. In other words, what happened?

This brings us to the dual nature of P/E. A low P/E means a stock may be an undiscovered value investment. *Or*, it may be discovered yet unappreciated.

I'd want a company with a low P/E to be a relatively new company with products or services that the market just doesn't know about or fully appreciate yet. A company that shows signs of being a coil ready to burst, with a beta higher than one and a market cap of mid cap or lower.

Target – which has been around for 100 years and appears to have already reached a mature/conservative stage – has a P/E of 14.19. Its P/E is relatively low compared to its industry's P/E of 56.06.

You can find a stock's industry P/E on Reuters. Just click "More from Reuters" under the Description on the stock's Google Finance homepage, click the "Financials" tab on the Reuter's page. Then, scroll down 1/3 of the way to the "Valuation Ratios" section.

Furthermore, back on Target's Google Finance homepage, if you look at the P/E for related companies (see the middle of the page, and click on each company's names to look at each P/E on their Google Finance homepages):

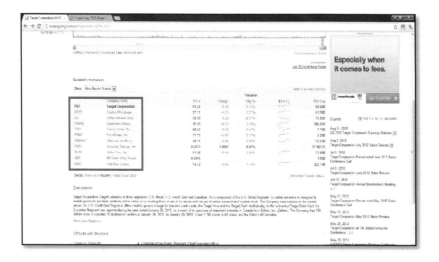

...you'll find other companies within the same industry as Target but with higher P/E's. In particular, Costco whose P/E is 27.1. And if you're like me, you really love the deals at Costco.

While Target's P/E may at first make it appear to be an undiscovered diamond in the rough, its P/E is not attractive after digging some more. Target may not be as valuable to investors as other stocks within its industry.

Step 6 Conclusion

Target does not appear to have a strong vote of confidence from investors. With Target being at a relatively mature stage, a low P/E relative to its industry average is a cause of concern to me.

Scorecard:

	PASSED?	SCORE
Step 1: Understand the Company's Business	✔	1
Step 2: Check the Price, and Evaluate the Price and Volume History	✔	1
Step 3: Check Style Fundamentals	✘	0
Step 4: Evaluate Sector and Industry Performance	✔	1
Step 5: Check Analyst Price Targets and Recent Headlines	✔	1
Step 6: Evaluate Market Share and Performance Relative to Competitors	✘	0
Step 7: Review Management Team and Management Effectiveness		
Step 8: Check Institutional Ownership		
Step 9: Analyze the Financials		
Step 10: Analyze the Technical Signals for Entry and Exit Points		
TOTAL		

Step 7: Review Management Team, and Management Effectiveness

How to Setup Your Browser for This Step:

➤ Return to Target's Homepage on Google Finance
➤ Scroll to the middle of the page to the section labeled "Officers and directors"

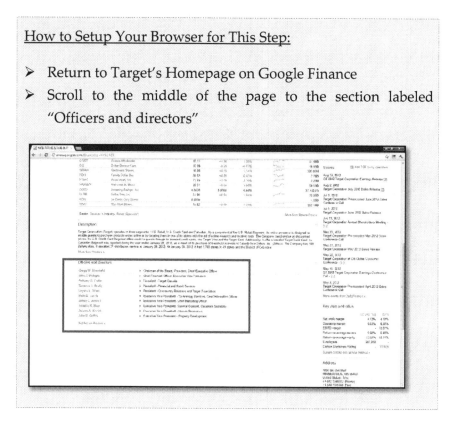

We can check if Target has the right captains at the helm by reviewing Target's management.

I look for the people at the top of a company to have at least 15 years of experience in the industry. They need deep, relevant experience so that they'll know the industry's challenges from an insider's point of view.

I also look for signs that top management connects with its customer base. For example, if the company sells golf clubs, does anyone in top management play golf?

A company gets a gold star if they have a diverse management team. They would only benefit from having multiple points of view and experiences.

Target's board appears to be young (the CEO is 57) but approximately the same age. It doesn't appear to be diverse.

I'm positive the majority of its shoppers are women, yet the top C-level positions are men. That's not a favorable sign to me. Do they know the deepest and most subtle wishes of its customers? Can they predict their customers' needs? Hmmm.

Management Effectiveness

In Your Browser...

➢ Return to Target's homepage on Google Finance
➢ Right above the "Officers and directors", click on the "More from Reuters" link
➢ On the Reuter's page, scroll approximately ¾ the way down the page to the "Management Effectiveness" section

These statistics tell investors whether the management team is running a lean and effective organization.

We want the stats for a company to be higher than the industry average. In particular, Return on Assets (ROA). This tells investors how effectively management uses its assets to make money.

Statistics like

"Return on Assets" allow investors to

analyze management's effectiveness.

For example, compare two plumbing companies that spent money on hammers. You would want to invest in the company that uses the hammers to build real estate and not toys (assuming real estate is a more profitable business than building toys).

ROA—like other numbers on this page—is a ratio, expressed as a percentage. Return on Assets specifically shows what percentage of the average cost of its assets is net profit – e.g.,

Net Profit / Average Cost of Company Assets = ROA

Target's ROA (6.59%) appears to be approximately its industry's ROA (6.27%). In fact, it is higher than Costco's ROA (which you can find by typing "COST" – Costco's ticker symbol – into the search field at the upper right hand corner of the Reuter's page).

This is a plus for Target!

Step 7 Conclusion

Target's management board lacks diversity. This makes me wonder if they can predict their customers' needs. Nevertheless, going by Target's ROA, they appear to be effective managers compared to their peers.

Scorecard:

	PASSED?	SCORE
Step 1: Understand the Company's Business	✔	1
Step 2: Check the Price, and Evaluate the Price and Volume History	✔	1
Step 3: Check Style Fundamentals	✘	0
Step 4: Evaluate Sector and Industry Performance	✔	1
Step 5: Check Analyst Price Targets and Recent Headlines	✔	1
Step 6: Evaluate Market Share and Performance Relative to Competitors	✘	0
Step 7: Review Management Team and Management Effectiveness	✔	1
Step 8: Check Institutional Ownership		
Step 9: Analyze the Financials		
Step 10: Analyze the Technical Signals for Entry and Exit Points		
TOTAL		

Step 8: Check Institutional Ownership

How to Setup Your Browser for This Step:

> Return to Target's Google Finance homepage
> Zero in on the statistics at the top of the page. You should see a percent value labeled "Inst. own". That is the value that we are going to discuss next.

Institutional ownership tells the percentage of a company's shares outstanding owned by professional investment organizations such as pension funds, mutual funds and hedge funds. These organizations pool together money from clients, and invest this money on their behalf into securities like stocks.

Institutions need to either make or preserve money for their clients. A high percentage of institutional ownership is a strong vote of confidence by the professional investment community.

Looking at institutional ownership requires the same point of view that you used when evaluating a company's P/E. Low institutional ownership is a positive when you're trying to find undiscovered companies. However, low institutional ownership with a mature company is a bad sign. Low to me is 50% or less.

We're considering Target to be, based on previous steps, a mature company. Its institutional ownership today is high (85%). That's a positive vote of confidence by the professional money management community.

Step 8 Conclusion

Institutions cannot risk too much of their clients' money by investing in a large number of high-flying, high-growth stocks. They may be using Target as a relatively stable dividend-earning place for portions of their portfolios. All in all, it's a good sign.

Scorecard:

	PASSED?	SCORE
Step 1: Understand the Company's Business	✓	1
Step 2: Check the Price, and Evaluate the Price and Volume History	✓	1
Step 3: Check Style Fundamentals	✗	0
Step 4: Evaluate Sector and Industry Performance	✓	1
Step 5: Check Analyst Price Targets and Recent Headlines	✓	1
Step 6: Evaluate Market Share and Performance Relative to Competitors	✗	0
Step 7: Review Management Team and Management Effectiveness	✓	1
Step 8: Check Institutional Ownership	✓	1
Step 9: Analyze the Financials		
Step 10: Analyze the Technical Signals for Entry and Exit Points		
TOTAL		

Step 9: Analyze the Financials

How to Setup Your Browser for This Step:

➤ Return to Target's Google Finance homepage
➤ Scroll down to the "Description" section, which describes the business.
➤ Click on the "More from Reuters" link below the Description paragraph. You should arrive at the stock's Reuter's homepage in another tab or browser window.
➤ Click on the "Financials" tab on the Reuter's homepage:

➤ Open another browser window (or press Ctrl-T to open another tab). In that tab, go to *http://finance.yahoo.com*
➤ Type in "TGT" (Target's symbol) in the search field underneath the "Home" tab on the left hand side of the page.
➤ Select "Target" from the dropdown field:

> ➤ On Yahoo!'s homepage for Target, scroll down until you reach the "Financials" section in the left hand side menu.
> ➤ Select "Income Statement" from the left hand side menu.

By this point, you probably already know whether you want to buy Target. If you do, you surely know the reasons why.

Regardless, your role in this process is like a coach during the draft process. You may hear of many great players and take a look at each to see what each does best. Once you find a player who performs a position well, you check the player's stats.

Checking stats verifies the player's skills before you actually draft him or her onto your team for that spot. You also look at stats to estimate how much the player is worth.

Target appears to be a candidate for a relatively stable, dividend-producing position in a portfolio. It's not necessarily the top performing company in its industry. However, it's appreciated by the professional community and has positive buzz in the media.

Sounds like we're about to draft a point guard! So let's take a look at Target's stats – e.g., "fundamentals" – to verify how well Target has performed with this role in mind.

Can an investor count on Target to have a stable price with steady earnings and reliable dividends? And how much should we really be paying for Target?

We're actually about to perform two types of fundamental analyses: "qualitative" and "quantitative".

With the qualitative review of Target's fundamentals, we're taking a peek under the hood of a company to perform a subjective "health check" on the business. Will we like the trends that we are seeing? Will we walk away feeling like Target has a strong, competitive future in this industry?

With the quantitative review, we use a company's fundamentals to estimate what its real stock price should be. If its estimated price is greater than the price that the stock trades at, we may have found an opportunity to buy a stock before the rest of the market catches on and drives up the market price.

Qualitative Analysis

Folks may try to make qualitative analysis sound like a mystical tea leaf-reading skill, but it's not. You just need common sense to assess the health of a business.

If you were a business owner performing a health check on your business, what would you ask yourself? The top four questions that I ask are:

➢ Is the business profitable?
➢ Does the business have a low amount of debt? If not, is the business able to repay its debts and is it using the money raised from incurring debt responsibly?
➢ Does the business have a competitive advantage, making it able to protect and defend its ability to make money in the future?
➢ Does anything look fraudulent about the financial statements?

Investing systems have been developed to create a process around performing this particular step – e.g., check for an increase in earnings over each of the past 5 years, etc. While a process is helpful as a guide, I've found that relying upon a process for a subjective analysis like this may make you jump to the wrong conclusion about a stock's health.

If you went to your doctor feeling tired, would you want your doctor to use the same checklist on you as he did for a child or a person of the opposite sex? No – you would want your doctor to ask you common sense questions tailored to your gender and age.

You'd also want the doctor to factor in your lifestyle and other "soft" factors. Otherwise, a child may be diagnosed as having too much stress in his life, and a woman may have a heart attack misdiagnosed.

*A good **qualitative analysis** checks a stock's performance **within the context of** its industry, sector, and the overall market's performances.*

As a result, how you answer questions during a qualitative analysis may vary depending on the performance of other things. For example, you wouldn't expect earnings for a company to continue to grow during a global economic downturn.

Therefore, if a company's earnings stalled during an overall bad time in the economy, that would not mean that the company is a bad investment.

This step involves a great deal of interpretation and a big picture (e.g., macro) perspective. As a result, don't get discouraged if you're not able to perform a qualitative analysis right away.

The first time you look at a company's financial statements, it'll just look like a bunch of numbers. But like most things in life, the more often you do it the more familiar the process will be.

Let's look at the Financials tab on Target's homepage on Reuters.

We know at this point that Target is in the "Retail (Specialty)" industry. What do you already know about this industry?

Looking at my own personal spending habits over the previous few years, I continued to buy new clothes despite the financial crisis and the recession. However, I and many other shoppers made an effort to look for ways to save money on new clothes.

Target, being a discount retailer for budget shoppers, could have seen an increase in sales.

Even if the industry as a whole had worse financials than usual because of the 2008 crisis, did more shoppers flock to Target over other discount retailers? Using my four common sense questions as a guide…

1. Is the business profitable?

On the Target homepage on Reuters on the Financial tab, scroll to the section called "Profitability Ratios":

PROFITABILITY RATIOS	Company	Industry	Sector
Gross Margin (TTM)	30.73	25.53	24.86
Gross Margin - 5 Yr. Avg.	30.50	24.87	24.71
EBITD Margin (TTM)	10.58	--	--
EBITD - 5 Yr. Avg	10.47	6.44	11.02
Operating Margin (TTM)	6.32	4.93	8.52
Operating Margin - 5 Yr. Avg	6.34	4.58	6.56
Pro Tax Margin (TTM)	6.32	4.65	10.13
Pre-Tax Margin - 5 Yr. Avg.	6.34	4.45	6.69
Net Profit Margin (TTM)	4.15	3.02	7.51
Net Profit Margin - 5 Yr. Avg.	4.05	2.89	4.82
Effective Tax Rate (TTM)	34.37	36.09	128.90
Effective Tax Rate - 5 Yr. Avg.	36.14	35.21	31.51
EFFICIENCY	Company	Industry	Sector
Revenue/Employee (TTM)	193,964	41,070,668	890,676,572
Net Income/Employee (TTM)	8,047	1,358,046	83,383,236
Receivable Turnover (TTM)	12.56	68.06	15.37
Inventory Turnover (TTM)	6.38	7.67	9.23

Underneath "Profitability Ratios", note the value for "Net Profit Margin (TTM)" (TTM means trailing twelve months, or "over the past 12 months"). The formula for this is:

Net Profit Margin = (Revenue - Expenses) / Revenue.

"Expenses" include the cost of the goods that Target sold, operating expenses and taxes. And a company's "revenue" is the money that they make from their products. You get "profit" by subtracting expenses from revenue.

Target had a higher net profit margin over the previous 12 months (4.15%) than the rest of the industry (3.02%). Looking at the 5-year average for Net Profit Margin, Target clobbered the industry (4.05% vs. 2.89%).

What Target's 4% Net Profit Margin tells you is for each $1 of revenue that Target makes, Target can make 4 cents of profit. For comparison, the average company in Target's industry and sector only make approximately 3 cents per dollar.

This may not sound like much. But Target is a large, expensive corporation. Either they are doing a better job than the rest of the industry with managing their expenses, or they're selling more products than other companies (or both).

Looking at Target's homepage on Yahoo! on its Income Statement page…

Income Statement		Get Income Statement for:		GO
View: Annual Data | Quarterly Data				All numbers in thousands
Period Ending	Jan 27, 2012	Jan 28, 2011	Jan 29, 2010	
Total Revenue	69,865,000	67,390,000	65,357,000	
Cost of Revenue	47,860,000	45,725,000	44,062,000	
Gross Profit	22,005,000	21,665,000	21,295,000	
Operating Expenses				
Research Development	-	-	-	
Selling General and Administrative	14,552,000	14,329,000	14,599,000	
Non Recurring	-	-	-	
Others	2,131,000	2,084,000	2,023,000	
Total Operating Expenses	-	-	-	
Operating Income or Loss	5,322,000	5,252,000	4,673,000	
Income from Continuing Operations				
Total Other Income/Expenses Net	3,000	3,000	3,000	
Earnings Before Interest And Taxes	5,325,000	5,255,000	4,676,000	
Interest Expense	869,000	760,000	804,000	
Income Before Tax	4,456,000	4,495,000	3,872,000	
Income Tax Expense	1,527,000	1,575,000	1,384,000	
Minority Interest	-	-	-	
Net Income From Continuing Ops	2,929,000	2,920,000	2,488,000	
Non-recurring Events				
Discontinued Operations	-	-	-	
Extraordinary Items	-	-	-	
Effect Of Accounting Changes	-	-	-	
Other Items	-	-	-	
Net Income	2,929,000	2,920,000	2,488,000	
Net Income Applicable To Common Shares	2,929,000	2,920,000	2,488,000	

...note the "Net Income Applicable to Common Shares" values at the very bottom of the page ($2.4B in 2010, $2.920B in 2011 and $2.929B in 2012). This shows us that Target's actual net income rose each year since 2010.

Relative to other companies in Target's industry and compared to previous years, Target appears to be in good shape in the profitability department.

2. Does the business have a low amount of debt? If not, is the business able to repay its debts and is it using the money raised from incurring debt responsibly?

On Reuter's homepage for Target on the "Financials" tab, scroll to the "Financial Strength" section. Note the values for:

➢ LT Debt to Equity Ratio (LT means long term): Any debt that a company does not expect to pay off in a year is long term debt. Types of long-term debt should sound familiar to you. These include leases or mortgages for offices/warehouses/land and business loans.

   A high ratio compared to the industry's ratio means that a company may be using more long-term debt (e.g., loans, etc.) to pay for its growth than other companies within its industry.

➢ Total Debt to Equity Ratio (MRQ) ("MRQ" means "most recent quarter". Note that January-March equals the first quarter of the year or Q1, April-June equals Q2, July-September equals Q3, and October-December equals Q4): Total debt includes short and long term debt. The definition is similar as the previous ratio, except this ratio also considers short-term debt (commercial paper, etc.).

➢ Current Ratio (MRQ): Calculated by dividing a company's assets by its current liabilities (e.g., short term debt). A ratio less than one means that a company owes more this year than it has the assets to sell off and pay for.

At the same time, a number that is too high (generally, over 3) may mean that the company is not investing in itself by buying assets/etc., and sitting on lazy cash that should be put to work.

➢ Quick Ratio (MRQ): Similar purpose as the Current Ratio – e.g., it tells you how quickly a company can sell the assets (e.g. equipment, shares that haven't been offered to the public yet, etc.) they own today to pay off their debts.

This ratio differs from the Current Ratio. This ratio doesn't include inventories (e.g., clothes/home goods/etc. waiting to be sold) as an asset.

Target's LT and Total debt to equity ratios (94.35% and 110% respectively) are much higher than the industry's LT and Total debt ratios (50.47% and 73.13% respectively).

Knowing at this point that Target is more profitable than the average company in its industry, Target may be using loans and other debt financing to fuel its growth.

Using loans is not a bad thing – unless Target becomes burdened by the dreaded interest payments. So let's check if

Target has enough assets to sell and generate cash if necessary to pay off its short and long term debts.

Targets current and quick ratios (1.25% and .64% respectively) are higher than the industry averages (1.07% and .46% respectively). A number over 1 is good – it means a company has enough assets to sell off and pay for its debt if it had to.

However, since Target's current ratio is higher than its quick ratio, and knowing that the quick ratio doesn't include inventories (e.g., clothes/home goods/etc. waiting to be sold), Target appears to have significant value in its inventory of goods waiting to be sold.

Since this is a retail industry, this isn't a surprise that Target may have significant inventory waiting to be sold. However, it is unnerving see that Target has a large percentage of loans compared to the rest of the industry.

3. Does the business have a competitive advantage, making it able to protect and defend its ability to make money in the future?

On a personal level, Target is definitely a go-to place for certain things. However, with so many new stores cropping up in the same niche, how has Target defended its position?

A company with a competitive advantage has:

➢ High Gross and Net Profit Margins: If you make a shirt for $10 and sell it for $50, your gross profit margin is $50-10 =

$40. Subtract interest payments, operating expenses and taxes and you'll get your net profit margin.

If you have to lower your sales price to get people to buy your shirt, you either have a product that isn't so popular or you've got competition (or both).

So a high profit margin usually means that the company has the freedom to charge as much as possible without having to compete on price, and their customers will pay for it because they have to have it. Think Apple.

➤ Consistent Gross and Net Profits: And ideally growing year after year.

We already know from the first question ("Is Target profitable?") that Target currently has a higher net profit margin than the industry average. Target's net income (e.g., net profit) has increased moderately over the previous three years. Its Gross Profit has also increased over 2010 ($21.2B), 2011 ($21.6B) and 2012 ($22B).

However, a general rule of thumb is if a company's gross profit margin is greater than 50% and net profit margin is over 20%, they have a competitive advantage.

For comparison, Apple has a gross profit margin today of approximately 44% and net profit margin of 27%. The average company in its industry has a gross profit margin of approximately 18% and net profit margin of 6%. Apple – with its iPads and other addictive products – has a massive competitive advantage!

Looking at Target's Reuters homepage under the "Profitability Ratios" section on the Financials tab, Target's gross profit margin is good: 30.73%. Its net profit margin – as we saw in step 1 – is 4.15%.

The Retail (Specialty) average gross profit margin is 25.53%, and average net profit margin is 3%.

While Target's gross profit margin has promise, it's not far off from the industry average. Also, Target's net profit margin definitely doesn't appear to reflect a competitive advantage.

Given that Target's industry competes on price and given that Target has a high percentage of debt, those factors may keep Target from acquiring unique products on which they can charge whatever price they want.

Which is a surprise – I love Target's collaborations with designers like Missoni, but I'm sure Target still can't charge its customers too much on those items either.

4. Does anything look fraudulent about the financial statements?

If in your gut you wondered "how is this company able to make money doing what they do", then this step would be pretty important towards trusting a company enough to invest.

Target has a clear strategy for making money – in particular, with its retail business.

You can go into any Target store, see customers buying things (things which Target likely bought wholesale at a lower price than what they're selling to customers), and understand that when Target makes a sale they get a cut of the proceeds.

Nevertheless, let's still perform this step. I don't suspect that Target needs to nor would pull shenanigans in their financial reports (unlike Enron and WorldCom).

Moreover, financial reporting regulations such as 2002's Sarbanes-Oxley Act aim to prevent fraudulent accounting, which damages investor confidence in the financial system. And we all know how shaky that confidence already is.

The great place to reference as we're completing this step is Target's homepage on Yahoo! Finance. Look at the menu on the left hand side, and scroll down to the "Financials" section. We'll use the Income and Cash Flow statements.

In general, your radar should go up if:

➢ Management compensation is heavily in stock, along with the CEO, CFO, or COO having an untrustworthy personality. These factors combined may give upper management reasons to drive up the stock price any way possible.

➢ The business model leaves you with questions or an uncomfortable feeling. Are you asking yourself "how can this company make money?"

➢ News stories come out about the company firing accountants, or about disorder amongst management or within the organization.

This may point to lax internal controls and discipline. Plus, how can a company be profitable for very long if they're a mess internally?

Once your antennae raises, three quick ways to spot fraud in the financial statements are:

➢ Inexplicably strong performance compared to other companies in the same industry
➢ Cash flow anomalies – in particular, a surge in the last quarter of the year
➢ Surges in sales/revenue – in particular, without an associated increase in accounts receivable.

From previous steps, we already know that Target's outperformance isn't extraordinary nor inexplicable.

The last two points above regarding cash flow anomalies and surges in sales and revenue involve analyzing Target's cash flow and income/balance statements.   Guidance on doing that analysis is beyond the scope of this book, and probably more effort than you have time to commit.

However, suffice it to say that if you read news stories questioning a company's accounting practices or questioning a company's business model even though the company meets earnings expectations each quarter, tread with caution.

Quantitative Analysis

A quantitative analysis is my favorite process for analyzing investments. Nothing is more conclusive than a number.

Remember Moneyball? Brad Pitt played a character that used numbers to determine which players to draft onto his team. The process of using numbers, calculations, and estimates to determine the worth of something is called "valuation".

Now, it is your turn to be Brad Pitt for a day.

In this stage, we're using numbers and other stats about stocks to determine a stock's fair value or "intrinsic value". You will not know if a stock's market price is too low and underappreciated until you estimate a stock's worth. Then you will know if you are getting a major league-quality stock for a minor league price.

But wait! Industry analysts have already done the dirty work for you. So use their estimates, even if you attempt to value a stock yourself.

USE THE WORK OF PROFESSIONAL ANALYSTS WHEN YOU ATTEMPT TO FIGURE OUT A STOCK'S INTRINSIC VALUE.

In Your Browser…

> Go to Target's Google Finance homepage
> Scroll to the bottom right hand corner.
> Click on "Analyst Estimates" under "External Links". You'll be taken to Target's homepage on MarketWatch.
> On MarketWatch's homepage for Target under "Snapshot", you'll see the "Average Target Price" that analysts calculated for Target. "Number of Ratings" tells you how many analysts made estimates.

Note that currently, the average target price shown on MarketWatch's site is $63.92. This average comes from the work of 26 analysts.

Keep in mind that a stock needs a track record in order for you to estimate its value. A rookie is harder to value than a mature player.

So if you're analyzing a stock that hasn't been public for more than 5-10 years, you may need to stick with analyst estimates.

Let's assume for a moment that you'd like to produce your own target price estimate.

If you do a Google search on "Stock Valuation", you'll find a dozen different ways to value a stock. Analysts tend to prefer the "discounted cash flow" method because it uses financials from a company that are hard for companies to manipulate with creative accounting methods.

This method estimates a company's current value based upon the cash it may generate in the future.

Discounted cash flow valuation may seem familiar. If you ever dated someone, you may have actually used this to rate the potential of a new girlfriend or boyfriend!

Note the word "estimates". One little word poses a huge hurdle. Knowing what to plug into the discount cash flow formula makes performing this (and any) valuation a challenge.

For example, the first step in performing this valuation involves estimating the cash a company may make each year over a 5 to 10-year period. In order to make that estimate, you have to factor in your opinion on a number of things that would affect the company's business.

This includes whether the company will continue to make sellable products, whether the company can gain or maintain its share of the market, whether the company can maintain or improve its gross margin. Not easy unless you're studying a company for a living.

Different assumptions will cause the valuation results to vary almost wildly. As a result, how to perform this type of estimate is outside the scope of this book.

Another alternative to using analyst estimates is using an interesting site called Trefis to dig into the factors that may affect a company's future business (and future stock price).

Go to _http://www.trefis.com_, type "Target" in the search field in the upper right hand corner, and select "Target" under Companies:

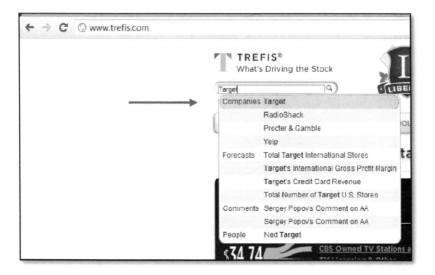

On the next page, you will see the "Trefis Price" (e.g., the estimate from analysts at Trefis), and you'll see how much each part of Target's business affects its stock price:

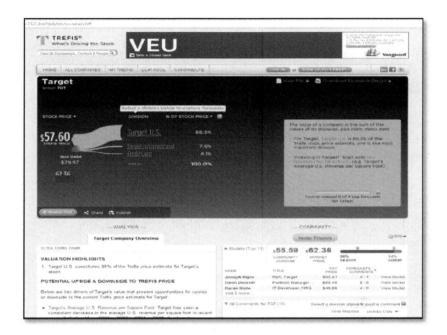

Trefis analysts believe that Target's fair stock price is lower than its current market value -- $57.60 vs. $61.52. In other words, Trefis analysts believe that Target's current market price may go down at some point in the future, and that it's overvalued by the stock market.

Under "Target Company Overview" on the lower left hand side, the analysts at Trefis give insights into what could cause Target's price to go up or down in the future.

For example, if Target could increase how much money they make per square foot in each US store to $350 per square foot, Target's stock price could rise by an estimated 10%!

The plus side of looking at this page is you can see the assumptions that Trefis analysts used, such as attributing 88.3% of Target's stock price to its US retail business.

You can also tweak their assumptions on the fly by clicking on each division and changing the forecasts as you see fit.

Be careful using the community opinions on the right hand side. Not all of these opinions come from professional stock analysts. Nevertheless, it's an interesting site for gaining insight into what may be driving a stock price. This insight may help you determine if a stock's current price may fall or rise in the future.

Conclusion for Step 9

While Target still appears to be a good stock compared to other companies in its industry, its business does not appear to be immune to competition.

Its stock price already trades near the target price estimated by analysts, and a large portion of its stock price depends on making sales from fickle retail consumers like you and me.

If Target paid a higher dividend (at least 3 – 3.5%, closer to the average rate of inflation), that would make up for owning a stock whose price may not rise much farther.

Scorecard:

	PASSED?	SCORE
Step 1: Understand the Company's Business	✔	1
Step 2: Check the Price, and Evaluate the Price and Volume History	✔	1
Step 3: Check Style Fundamentals	✘	0
Step 4: Evaluate Sector and Industry Performance	✔	1
Step 5: Check Analyst Price Targets and Recent Headlines	✔	1
Step 6: Evaluate Market Share and Performance Relative to Competitors	✘	0
Step 7: Review Management Team and Management Effectiveness	✔	1
Step 8: Check Institutional Ownership	✔	1
Step 9: Analyze the Financials	✘	0
Step 10: Analyze the Technical Signals for Entry and Exit Points		
TOTAL		

Step 10:   Analyze the Technical Signals for Entry and Exit Points

How to Setup Your Browser for This Step:

➢ Go to Google's homepage for Target at http://finance.google.com

➢ Zero in on the chart area. Select "Technicals" underneath the chart:

➢ Select "Simple Moving Average (SMA)" in the first pulldown list, and use a 50-day period (e.g., type the number 50 in the box to the left of "Period").

➢ If necessary, click the "Add technical" link to get another pulldown list.

➢ Select "Simple Moving Average (SMA)" from the next pulldown list, and use a 200-day period.

➢ If necessary, click the "Add technical" link to get another pulldown list.

➢ Select "Relative Strength Index (RSI)" from the third pulldown list, and use a 14-day period.

Target has three strikes on its scorecard. If this were the Olympic Games, Target would be in fourth place.

This does not mean Target isn't a good investment. With 85% of its stock owned by institutions, Target has a solid vote of confidence from the investment community.

Nevertheless, you will probably have a much smaller portfolio than a hedge fund or pension fund. So Target could make up a significant part of your portfolio – perhaps the only representative from its industry.

As a result, you would want the very best in price and/or dividend potential. Based on our analysis, Target may not be the best candidate for a small portfolio. In other words, it still appears to be a bread-and-butter point guard that needs a strong team around it.

Nevertheless, let's assume for a moment you want to buy Target. Would now be the best time to buy? Is Target's stock in a position to buy, or will its price will fall soon?

What we're about to do is called a "technical analysis". The financial community considers it to be the opposite of a fundamental analysis. We're looking at outward signals of a stock to determine which way it may move in the near term.

We want to avoid buying a stock right before the price declines. Looking at its technicals may help us assess timing.

It's like placing your hand on a child's forehead to determine if he or she has a fever, versus using a thermometer to take his or her temperature from the inside.

Together, both fundamental and technical analyses provide a full picture of the health of a stock.

Depending on whether you are a short or long-term investor, you may emphasize doing a technical analysis over a fundamental analysis.

This book focuses on long term investing – which places more emphasis on finding value instead of finding a trend. In other words, this book places more emphasis on using the results of a fundamental analysis of a stock.

Nevertheless, I wouldn't want to buy a stock without checking whether the price may fall soon.

As a result, when I check a stock's technicals, I'm checking to see that the stock's price is trending upward. If it's not trending upwards, I'm checking if the price has "support" or a floor within 10% below where its current price.

What are Examples of Technical Signals?

I can't begin to describe the long list of technical signals that investors and traders use. Generally, the types of signals fall in the following three categories:

➤ Trend Indicators: Measure the overall direction of a price
➤ Breadth Indicators: Measure the strength of a trend
➤ Oscillators: Measure trend and breadth

No one technical signal can confirm anything. Traders and investors use a handful of indicators that have worked for them in the past, and only act if all of their indicators support a buy or a sell.

I have three indicators that I like using. Institutional investors also use these. As mentioned in Step 2, institutions have the power to move the market with their large trades. Knowing whether they will buy or sell can only help you as an individual investor to ride their trend wave.

50-Day and 200-Day Simple Moving Average Charts

A moving average takes the average price over a previous period, and plots it into one point. Each point on a moving average chart, as a result, is the average of several points in the past.

On a 50-day moving average chart, each point averages the closing prices of a stock over the previous 50 days. And on a 200-day moving average chart, each point averages the closing prices of a stock over the previous 200 days. The results are charts that help you clearly see stock price trends.

For example, imagine if you had to explain whether your income has increased over the previous three years. You may instantly compare annual numbers – e.g., $75K in year one vs. $80K in year two vs. $90K in year three.

However, imagine trying to see a trend in daily numbers – e.g., $300 on January 2nd vs. $300.03 on January 3rd vs. $300.02 on January 4th, and so on.

Looking at a longer timeframe helps you see a trend more clearly. It would be a nightmare trying to see a trend in daily stock prices. As a result, the moving average helps tremendously in seeing price trends over various periods of time.

Other flavors of moving average charts exist – such as smoothed and exponential. However, the simple moving average is simply an easy way to look at a stock's trend.

Keep in mind that since these use previous prices, these charts show trends that are currently forming, and not future trends. So once you spot an opportunity (and I will show you how), you have to act quickly.

The 50-day chart reflects the stock's short-term trend or momentum, and the 200-day chart reflects the stock's long-term trend or momentum. The shorter the time frame, the more sensitive the chart is to a trend that is forming today.

If you're looking at both the 50-day and 200-day charts together, you'll see moments when the 50-day chart crosses the 200-day. Let's see an example of this on Target's chart.

The left arrow is pointing to the 50-day moving average, and the right arrow points to the 200-day moving average. The jagged line is the plot of Target's daily closing prices:

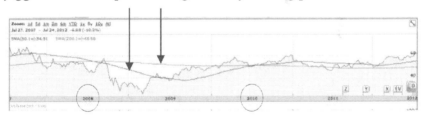

A crossing means optimism or pessimism is taking control of the price. When the 50-day line crosses below the 200-day line (which happened for Target in 2008), traders are becoming pessimistic about a stock and are selling. When the 50-day line crosses above the 200-day line (which happened in 2010), traders are being optimistic about a stock and are buying.

Let's zero-in on Target's chart over since late 2010:

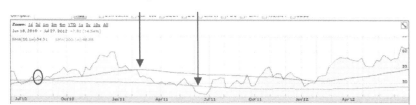

The left arrow is points to the 50-day line, and the right points to the 200-day line.

The 50-day moving average line has been above the 200-day moving average line since August 2010. So it appears traders and investors may have been optimistic about Target since then!

But how much oomph does that optimism have? Will the optimism fade soon?

Relative Strength Indicator (RSI)

An oscillator indicator like the relative strength indicator tells traders and investors whether a trend may fade or pick up steam.

Just like a swimmer, a stock needs to regroup or take a breath occasionally. RSI, in essence, measures when a stock needs to take a breath.

If investors have bought a stock repeatedly (driving up a price), the time will come when the stock takes a breath and its price declines. This occurs for various reasons, including when traders sell and claim their profits.

RSI helps investors estimate when a stock could be ready to take a "breath" due to being overbought (e.g., too high in price), or ready to rise back up in price due to being oversold.

Let's add RSI to Target's chart since late 2010:

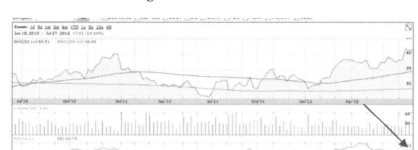

The bottom chart is Target's RSI. Note that investors consider a stock to be overbought when RSI rises above 70, and oversold when RSI falls below 30.

Notice how the RSI chart line is starting to increase on the far right corner, but is not at a peak yet. This means that Target's stock may not have peaked yet, and still may be at a decent price to buy.

But when Target's price starts to "take a breath" and fall, how far might it fall?

Fibonacci Retracements

"Fibonacci" may sound like an Italian Renaissance painter. When a trader or investor draws Fibonacci Retracements on a stock's price chart, he or she can see the most likely points where a stock's price has support (e.g., where a stock's price stops going lower) or resistance (e.g., where a stock's price stops going higher).

When a stock's price "takes a breath", this technical charting technique assumes that the price will fall back to one of many specific levels, and then either rebound or continue to fall.

It's a fascinating technique that I've actually seen work. It originated with Leonardo Fibonacci in 1202, when he discovered a unique numerical pattern. Each successive number in the pattern is the sum of the previous two numbers:

0, 1, 1, 2, 3, 5, 8, 13, 21, 34, 55, 89, and so on

By dividing certain numbers by others, you get a set of ratios. For example, by dividing any number after the 1's by the number that follows it, and you will get approximately 0.618, or 61.8%. All of the "golden ratios" are:

0%, 23.6%, 38.2%, 50%, 61.8%, 78.6%, and 100%

These ratios appear in finance, and even in nature. For example, your elbow rests 61.8% the way down your arm. And 61.8% of the distance between your head and your feet is your belly button!

In the stock market, after a stock's price increases for a period, its price may decline to a level either 23.6% below its high, or 38.2% below, or 50% below, and so on before rebounding.

And vice versa – after a stock's price decreases for a period, its price may increase to a level either 23.6% higher, or 38.2% higher, or 50% higher, and so on before going back down again.

If a stock's price rises or falls past a level, it may either hit the next level before reversing, or continue its original trajectory. In particular, if the price breaks through the 50% level, traders and investors believe a stock's price will continue its trajectory.

Each level is psychologically significant, and acts as a decision point as to which direction a stock will take. Since many investors trade by these levels, it's a great way to get into the same mindset as them.

Using Fibonacci Retracements

Let's look at Target's chart. First, identify a clear trend followed by a clear reversal. Target's last clear trend occurred when its price declined between July 13, 2007 (when it hit a high of $70.14) and March 6, 2009 (when it hit a low of $25.65). A reversal back up followed:

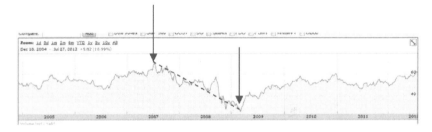

On a chart, you would draw a line between the two trend points like the dashed line that I drew above.

Next, calculate the distance between these two points: $70.14 - $25.65 = $44.49.

Finally, calculate the values at the golden ratios. With a downward trend like the one above, you will be calculating how far the price will *rise* before it may reverse down.

Notice that I said "may". Each retracement level is a decision point where the price may or may not reverse. The higher the ratio, the less likely the price may reverse.

So on this chart, the levels at which the price will likely stop rising are:

Low Price + (Distance x Ratio) = Level

$25.65 + ($44.49 x 23.6%) = $36.15

$25.65 + ($44.49 x 38.2%) = $42.65

$25.65 + ($44.49 x 50%) = $47.90

$25.65 + ($44.49 x 61.8%) = $53.14

$25.65 + (44.49 x 78.6%) = $60.62

$25.65 + ($44.49 x 100%) = $70.14

Using other technical indicators like RSI and the SMA charts may help figure out whether the stock's price has the momentum to keep rising, or if the momentum will stop because the stock is overbought.

Note the opposite situation. If we were looking at a rising trend, you would calculate the levels at which the price would *fall* and before it may reverse back up. The levels would be calculated as:

High Price - (Distance x Ratio) = Level

On a price chart, you would draw horizontal lines at the levels so that you could clearly see when the price chart reverses or breaks through a level.

Notice the two levels drawn below – the 50% (e.g., $47.90) and the 78.6% (e.g., $60.62) levels.

The chart passed all levels – including the 50% level. It rose to the 78.6% level before reversing again. It met support at the 50% level before continuing back up. This supports the theory that if the stock price crosses the 50% level on its way back up or back down, it'll likely meet support there and continue its trajectory.

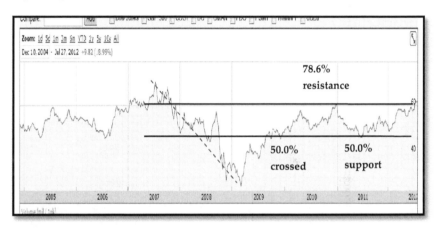

When I first saw this happen on a stock's chart, I thought it was magical. I continue to think that today!

Conclusion for Step 10

Target's price appears to be in a position to keep rising. But it's awfully close to running out of steam!

Scorecard:

	PASSED?	SCORE
Step 1: Understand the Company' s Business	✔	1
Step 2: Check the Price, and Evaluate the Price and Volume History	✔	1
Step 3: Check Style Fundamentals	✘	0
Step 4: Evaluate Sector and Industry Performance	✔	1
Step 5: Check Analyst Price Targets and Recent Headlines	✔	1
Step 6: Evaluate Market Share and Performance Relative to Competitors	✘	0
Step 7: Review Management Team and Management Effectiveness	✔	1
Step 8: Check Institutional Ownership	✔	1
Step 9: Analyze the Financials	✘	0
Step 10: Analyze the Technical Signals for Entry and Exit Points	✔	1
TOTAL		**7**

Congratulations! You completed a 10-step evaluation of a stock! Target appears to be right on the edge of being a slam-dunk buy for a portfolio. However, it scored in a range where I would put it on a watch list. If its performance and/or financials improve, it will become, in my opinion, a strong buy for an individual investor's portfolio.

What If You Don't Have a Clue?

What if you don't have any stock ideas, or if you don't have the time to do all of these research steps? I have two more options for you.

You can subscribe to a research service from a reputable company. For example, Morningstar covers 1700 stocks. They list all of the stock that they follow at:

http://www.morningstar.com/analyst-research/stock-reports.aspx

You can either look at their list and narrow it down using your own research, or purchase a report. This is not an endorsement of Morningstar's research. However, I use Morningstar's Advisor tools and feel the company produces high-quality products for investors.

You can also create an Excel workbook to "mine the stock market for gold". I recommend this for advanced Excel users.

First, download a symbol list from End of Day Data: http://eoddata.com. You can download all of the symbols in the S&P 500 and other indices for free.

Next, install the Stock Market Functions Add-in written by Randy Harmelink from:

http://finance.groups.yahoo.com/group/smf_addin/

If you place the list of symbols into Excel, you can use this add-in to download stock market data into your workbook. You can download prices and even fundamentals like P/E.

Next, add a rule under "Conditional Formatting" to highlight a cell if it passes one of your checks. For example, if a stock's last close price is less than an analyst's target price, highlight that price cell green. However, if the stock's last close price is close to its target price, highlight the cell yellow. And if it's over, highlight it red (or not at all).

You will end up with a dashboard like the snapshot below. If you create a workbook based off the 10-step research process and if a stock has more than 8 cells green, you can quickly see that it passed enough checks to qualify for your portfolio.

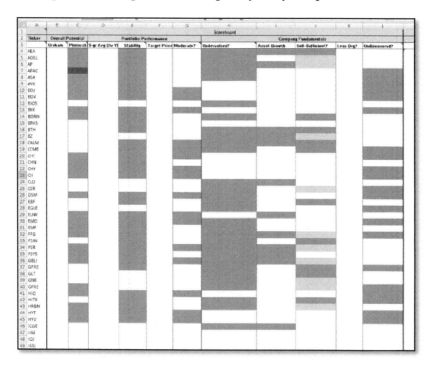

WORKBOOK GUIDE: ENTER YOUR SCORE ON THE "MY STOCK RESEARCH" TAB IN THE "MY RESEARCH SCORE" COLUMN. THEN, REPEAT THE 10-STEP RESEARCH PROCESS FOR EACH PRODUCT THAT YOU LIKE!

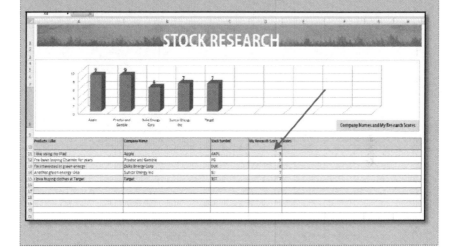

Key Takeaways

✓ Always start your list of investment ideas with companies that make products you love. You'll have a head start in understanding that company's business.

✓ Google, Yahoo!, and other sites provide incredible resources for researching a stock for free.

✓ Following the 10-step research process in this chapter will help you analyze all factors that affect a stock's price.

✓ Researching a stock may take a while at first. However, it may eventually take you less than 10-15 minutes per stock once you become familiar with the process.

Another key takeaway: I am proud of you for making it this far. Keep reading!

STEP 5: CREATE A

PORTFOLIO

Investors' portfolios may only come second in size and importance their house!

Assets like a house and a stock portfolio support their owner – whether by providing a secure place to live, or a protective cushion of money. We would naturally want something that supports us to be as stable as possible.

Think about buying a chair. Would you buy a chair with one leg or four? Wouldn't you want a chair with more than one leg so you don't tip over? Or would you be willing to risk owning a chair with too few legs to make it stable?

It makes sense to check stability and risk when you buy a chair. Then why don't investors consider this when they put money into one of things that could support them the most?

Why Investors Don't Think About Creating Portfolios

Creating a balanced, diversified portfolio takes understanding unfamiliar things like "exposure", "risk", "weighting", and "return". As a result, individuals sometimes avoid studying those things before rushing to feel the excitement of owning a hot stock.

I don't blame you. It's like buying candy. When you want the peppermint, you want it. You don't want to think about the cotton candy you had for breakfast, or the chocolate cake you're planning to have for dinner.

Only after you've gone through the experience of having heartburn and cavities will you realize that looking at the big picture helps. As a result, you start to recall lessons about "calories", "saturated fat", and "cholesterol" before snacking on pizza at work and finishing it off with a piece of birthday cake.

Stocks give the same kind of sugar rush. However, just like putting candy into your body, you cannot put stocks into your portfolio over the long term without considering your portfolio's overall health.

Maximum Pleasure, Minimum Risk

Speaking of chocolate cake, wouldn't it be great if we could have it all the time? If we could enjoy a cool plate in the morning with milk, and a warm delicious plate for dinner?

Unfortunately, our bodies would shut down after a while if we did that. So what do we do instead? We'll have a piece of chocolate cake just once a week. Or – if you're like me – eat a whole cake over Thanksgiving weekend and call it a day until the next year.

This strategy balances the pleasure of eating chocolate cake with the risk of harming our health. In other words, we are maximizing pleasure while minimizing risk.

You can apply the same strategy to your portfolio. Buying aggressive, high-flying stocks may put you in a position to make as much money as possible. However, the stocks that have the potential to give you the greatest return also tend to be risky.

What if you could maximize your portfolio's growth while minimizing your portfolio's risk? You would not only control how much money you make, but also the danger of losing all of your money. As a result, you would have all of the pleasure of making money without the agony of losing it all.

The 2008 global financial crisis brought "portfolio risk management" into the vocabulary of individual investors. What does it really mean, and how do you "manage the risk of your portfolio"?

Modern Portfolio Theory

The cradle of managing portfolio risk rests under something called "modern portfolio theory". Harry Markowitz developed the theory in 1952. Although 1952 isn't all that modern, parts of this theory still haven't made it into the everyday investment habits of individuals.

Modern portfolio theory says investing isn't just about picking stocks. It's also about picking the right combination of stocks. The right combination will maximize your portfolio return year after year, while reducing the risk of losing money.

Markowitz didn't just pull this theory out of the air. It's actually *mathematically* true that you can change how risky your portfolio is by changing the proportions of the same set of stocks.

Think about a football team. If you're a risky coach, you may play your aggressive quarterback more often. He may always try to throw a touchdown passes. His aggressive style matches the coach's risk profile.

On the other hand, if you're a conservative coach you may play a conservative quarterback more often. This quarterback may hand the ball to other players instead of throwing it.

Coaches will use players in different proportions to change their teams' performances to their liking. It's similar to how a person who desires a risky portfolio may aim for a higher proportion of risky stocks.

Modern Portfolio Theory shows investors how to adjust their stock choices and share proportions in a portfolio with risk in mind. However, I recommend using Modern Portfolio Theory techniques as just a guide. You'll ultimately need to decide the final proportions that work best for your situation.

The following two areas in Modern Portfolio Theory stick out as important areas to consider when you build and manage a portfolio.

Correlation

If it always rains in Southern California when your children go outside to play, Southern California rain correlates to your children's playtime.

Correlation means two things have a relationship. The relationship may be positive – for example, children who play instruments also have high grades. The relationship could also be negative – when your spouse eats, you're stuck doing the dishes.

Stocks in your portfolio can also have a relationship. Your job is to identify and manage those relationships to your benefit.

Each stock in your portfolio represents a country, sector, or industry. None of these areas pays off year after year. Instead, each pays off in a cycle where some years are great, and some are not.

Correlated stocks have a **relationship.**

The relationship may be

positive or negative.

Your job is to **manage** *those relationships.*

As a portfolio manager, you encourage positive relationships if you feel an industry, sector, or country may have a great year. However, if a stock may have a bad year, you may add another stock to your portfolio with a negative relationship to counterbalance it.

For example, let's assume that you have Target in your portfolio. We researched Target in the last step, prior to this chapter.

Let's also assume that Target performs well during a recession because shoppers seek out Target's sales.

You feel confident that this area of the market will outperform. You then decide that you would like to take advantage of this atmosphere. Subsequently, you may seek out stocks that have a positive correlation to Target.

For example, stocks in the same industry as Target will likely positively correlate with Target. Also, stocks from companies that create products for the same type of customer that shops at Target may trend the same way too.

However, take care with this portfolio. When the market turns around, you don't want the stocks in your portfolio to decline at the same time. As a result, if more than one of your stocks has the same:

- ✓ Industry
- ✓ Sector
- ✓ Market Capitalization (e.g., Style)
- ✓ Country of Business

...watch out if either of these areas has a bad year. Since a bad year may be tough to predict, try to diversify your stock portfolio across these factors. Especially if you're not confident in knowing when each area will outperform.

EVEN STOCKS HAVE RELATIONSHIPS, AND MOVE IN CONCERT. IT IS YOUR JOB TO RECOGNIZE AND MANAGE THOSE RELATIONSHIPS SO THAT YOUR STOCKS COEXIST IN PEACE!

An Advanced Look at Correlation

If you would like to take analyzing correlation to the next level, use Excel and historical prices to check how correlated two stocks may be.

First, download historical prices for your stocks at either Google Finance, or Yahoo! Finance. Let's use Google Finance as an example.

Go to http://finance.google.com and search for each stock by symbol or company name:

After clicking on the search result, you'll be taken to that stock's Google Finance homepage.

Next, click on "Historical Prices" in the left hand side menu:

On the next page, you'll see historical prices for your stock. Click the "Download to workbook" link on the right hand side. Repeat these steps for your second stock. Ensure that you export the same date range for both stocks.

Create a workbook with the Close prices for both of your stocks in side-by-side columns:

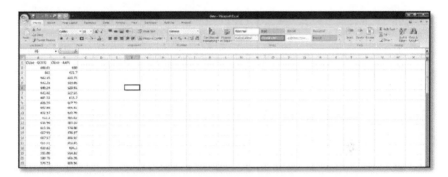

Next, use Excel's "CORREL" formula to determine the correlation between these two columns:

=CORREL(array1, array2)

Use the following as a guide to determine your stocks' correlation:

-1 = Perfectly NEGATIVELY correlated

0 = No Correlation

1 = Perfectly POSITIVELY correlated

I checked Apple and Google's correlation, and got "0.428". This means they are positively correlated, but not strongly.

Target Portfolio Return

In Step 3 when we discussed goal-based investing, the four pieces you figured out for each goal were:

- ✓ Your purpose for investing
- ✓ Your destination lifestyle
- ✓ Your timeframe to invest
- ✓ How much you can invest on a monthly basis

In Step 4, we researched your stock ideas.

Now that you have a list of stocks and your mini-financial plan, are you ready to buy?

Not yet. You need to know how much of each stock to buy. In order to figure that out, you need to know the proportion of each stock you need in order to reach your destination.

It's our football coach example all over again. What proportion of each player in your portfolio does it take to win?

Remember when we determined whether you were saving enough for each goal? If you're using the workbook, the workbook estimated the average annual portfolio return that you needed to hit your goal on the "My Goals" tab:

The last column on the "My Goals" tab gives an estimated target portfolio return for each of your goals.

You can actually use this estimate as a guide to help you figure out how many shares of each stock you may need to buy in your portfolio.

Just like players on a team, each stock has its own stats. The coach determines playing time based upon the needs of the team. If the coach needs an aggressive team, for example, he will put a higher percentage of aggressive players into the game.

Each stock has its own average annual return. Each stock also has its own degree of risk. Using both of these stats together, you can aim for a target portfolio return while minimizing your risk. We'll cover how in the next section.

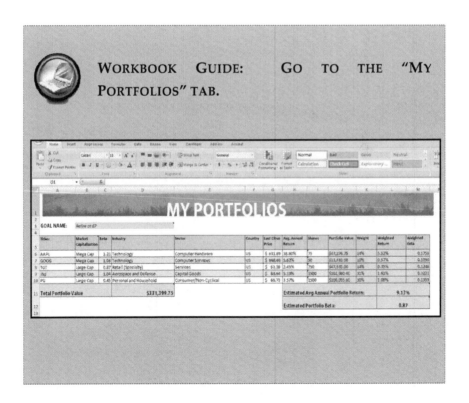

WORKBOOK GUIDE: GO TO THE "MY PORTFOLIOS" TAB.

Build Your Portfolio

When you build a stock portfolio using the right principles, it may feel as if you are juggling while ice skating.

You're not only building a team of stocks that will give you the portfolio return you need, but the stocks also need to be diversified (depending on your confidence in knowing which areas of the market will outperform) and not highly correlated.

As a result, let's step carefully through each key area needed to build a portfolio.

Risk Pyramid

To start, a simple guideline for building your portfolio would be to use a style pyramid like the below:

**Aggressive Stocks:
Typically Small Cap or
less, and Beta over 2**

**Moderate Stocks: Typically
Small to Mid Cap, and Beta
between 1-2**

**Conservative Stocks: Typically Large to
Mega Cap, and Beta less than 1**

In other words, manage your risk by minimizing your proportion of aggressive stocks.

This pyramid assumes that you have cash savings in another account. Remember, do not invest all of your savings. Ensure that you have emergency savings in cash or an equivalent (e.g., Money Market, CD, etc.). Speak with an advisor you know and trust to determine the right amount of savings for your situation.

Based on your research in the last section, how do your stock ideas fall amongst these areas? Do you primarily have Small Cap stocks? Or the reverse?

Keep in mind that the more stocks that you have in your portfolio that land at the top of the pyramid, the more raucous your ride may be in the stock market.

Diversification

As mentioned in the previous section, attempt to diversify on the following areas. You can use Google Finance to find all of these values:

➢ Industry
➢ Sector
➢ Style (e.g., Market Cap and Beta)
➢ Country of Business: Use the business' description on Google Finance or Trefis to determine the country where it receives the most revenue. A stock may be incorporated in the US, yet may be receiving strong revenue from overseas.

Overall Portfolio Return

In Step 2, you may have determined the target return that your portfolio needed to hit each of your goals. Next, we will figure out whether your stock ideas will get you to that target return.

A simple method for estimating your portfolio's average annual return is to do a "weighted aggregation". In other words:

1.   First, estimate each stock's average annual return.

     For this part, we will use each stock's actual average historical return. Please keep in mind that past performance does not dictate future performance. Also, keep in mind that the 2008 financial system collapse caused historical returns to skew lower than normal.

     You can find a stock's average annual return at Morningstar.

     ➢ Go to http://www.morningstar.com
     ➢ In the Quote box at the top of the page, enter your symbol:

     ➢ Once you get to the next page, click on "Performance" in the middle of the page.
     ➢ Scroll to the bottom of the page. Look for the 5-Year, or 10-Year, or 15-Year Total Return %.

Note that there are different schools of thought as to which return to use. In my opinion, use the same maximum timeframe for each of your stocks. For example, if each of your stocks has a 5-Year value on Morningstar, use it. However, if each has a greater timeframe, use it.

Total Return % (08/14/2012)	1-Day	1-Week	1-Month	3-Month	YTD	1-Year	3-Year	5-Year	10-Year	15-Year
GOOG	1.95	2.95	15.58	18.73	7.57	18.68	13.28	5.63	—	—
Internet Content & Information	1.17	0.73	3.18	-6.17	-7.79	-7.64	6.89	3.59	27.11	21.18
S&P 500 TR	0.09	0.30	3.68	5.52	13.16	21.81	14.17	3.90	6.44	4.58
+/- Internet Content & Information	0.14	3.86	12.80	26.87	15.25	26.45	6.40	4.60	—	—
+/- S&P 500 TR	1.91	-4.06	12.10	5.19	-4.64	5.21	-0.89	3.71	—	—

2. Multiply each stock's average annual return by its weight in your portfolio.

I recommend weighting by the stock's percentage of the total value of your portfolio. For example, if your total portfolio value is $5000 and if a stock makes up $1200 of that total, that stock's weight is $1200/$5000 = 24% of your portfolio.

3. Add together each stock's weighted return to get an estimate for your portfolio's total average annual return.

WORKBOOK GUIDE: SAVE YOURSELF SOME PAIN. THE WORKBOOK CALCULATES THIS FOR YOU ON THE "MY PORTFOLIOS" TAB.

Tweak your shares until you reach your portfolio's target return from the "My Goals" tab. You may even realize you need different stocks in order to reach your target return. If that is the case, please continue your research for additional stocks, and keep trying.

Please remember to speak with a professional before you invest. The above is simply an estimate.

To Guess Your Number of Shares or Not to Guess

In the last step, we guessed at how many shares we needed to buy of each stock. If you're like me, you probably feel uncomfortable guessing at anything involving where your money is going to go.

What if you could figure out exactly how many shares you needed to buy to not only make the return that you need, but also at the least amount of risk? In other words, how can you actually maximize your pleasure while minimizing your pain from potentially losing money? And to do it without guessing?

The Efficient Frontier solves this problem.

It may sound like a Naked Gun-style adventure movie from the 80's. Actually, it's a mathematical way to find the optimal share proportions giving the highest return with minimum risk.

In other words given a list of stocks, the Efficient Frontier will tell you the exact number of shares of each that you should buy in order to maximize your returns while minimizing your risk.

You will likely have to modify your share amounts after using the Efficient Frontier. However, it is a good guide for figuring out the ballpark proportions of stocks that you need to minimize your risk.

Using the Efficient Frontier is outside of the scope of this book. However, if you subscribed to Modern Wealth Media's blog, you may get an article about this in your mailbox in the future.

What About Bonds and Other Types of Investments?

Other types of investments will definitely provide you with the diversification you need to get steadier returns than with stocks alone.

If you are interested in adding other types of investments into your portfolio, you can use the chart below as a guide:

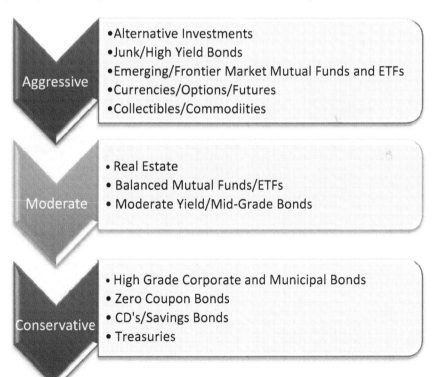

Aggressive
- •Alternative Investments
- •Junk/High Yield Bonds
- •Emerging/Frontier Market Mutual Funds and ETFs
- •Currencies/Options/Futures
- •Collectibles/Commodiities

Moderate
- • Real Estate
- • Balanced Mutual Funds/ETFs
- • Moderate Yield/Mid-Grade Bonds

Conservative
- • High Grade Corporate and Municipal Bonds
- • Zero Coupon Bonds
- • CD's/Savings Bonds
- • Treasuries

Also, annuities if appropriate may be used to create your own "pension plan" from a 401K rollover. This is not a recommendation or offer to buy annuities, and keep in mind the suitability of annuities before you buy.

Please keep in mind you should research each investment before adding it into your portfolio. The chart is not a recommendation to buy or sell any particular security. Moreover, as always, speak with a professional that you know and trust before investing.

Key Takeaways:

✓ Modern Portfolio Theory can guide you on picking the right proportion of stocks to maximize your portfolio's return while minimizing your risk of losing your money.

✓ Lowering your stocks' correlations and aiming for a target return dictate which stocks you decide to invest in and how much of each.

✓ Add the value-weighted historical returns to estimate your portfolio's overall historical return. If you're ambitious, use the Efficient Frontier to take the guesswork out of how many shares of each stock you should buy in your stock portfolio in order to hit a target return with minimum risk.

✓ Other types of investments besides stocks may be added to your portfolio to help you meet a target return. Speak with a professional that you know and trust to discuss what is appropriate for your situation.

STEP 6: DETERMINE HOW MUCH MONEY YOU ARE WILLING TO LOSE...OR GAIN

The 1990's spoiled investors. Not only could any software developer and his or her cousin write a business plan on a napkin and take a company public, but that company's stock price would double or triple on nothing but hype.

As a result, many investors forgot how the market really works. It goes up AND it goes down (not just up). As 2008 taught us, the market sometimes can keep going down without going back up again for a long time.

Smart investors understand

that they may lose money.

So smart investors plan ahead,

and know how much they are able to lose

before they have to sell.

A smart investor buys stocks knowing he or she can lose money. In fact, you will lose money. Let me repeat – you WILL lose money when you invest in stocks.

If you picked great investments, you will make your money back and then some when your stock rebounds. Nevertheless, you may have a situation where your stock is not rebounding for an extended period. Like 2008.

Way before you get to that point – even before you buy the stock – you have to ask yourself how much money are you able to lose before selling out of your position.

Making Up for Lost Money

Consider an investor named Hugh J. Loss who stayed in the market during the tumultuous summer of 2011 with a portfolio that tracked the S&P 500:

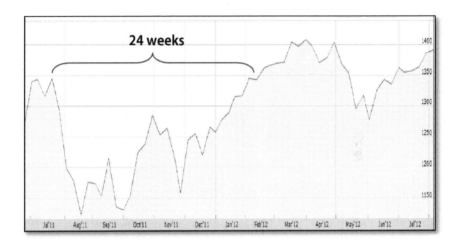

First, the market dropped 13% between July 22 and August 10, 2011. Subsequently, it took Hugh J. Loss 24 weeks to recover before his portfolio started to make money again. That is six months of just getting back to where he began on July 22.

I hope Hugh knew on July 22 whether he could survive a 13% loss without having to adjust his timeframe or destination goal amount. Otherwise, Hugh thinks ahead no more than a beachgoer who swims far into the ocean before realizing he is too tired to swim back.

As a smart investor, you have to plan several steps ahead and know when to hold, and when to fold.

Managing Portfolio Losses

Let's look at another investor: Ivana B. Retired.

Ivana is 58 years old and has a timeline of 9 years before she starts living off her investments. She doesn't like taking risks.

She currently has an IRA (individual retirement account) that she estimates has an average annual historical return of 9%. She plans to switch to a 6% return with more conservative investments 3 years before retirement begins.

Since Ivana is over 50, she can contribute $6000/year into her IRA as of 2012. As a result, she contributes $500/month (which totals to $6000/year).

Her portfolio now has $350,000, and she wants to retire with $750,000 in investments.

How big of a loss can her portfolio take before she is unable to hit her goal amount in 7 years?

IF YOU'RE LIKE IVANA B. RETIRED, TRY TO FIGURE OUT HOW MUCH YOUR PORTFOLIO CAN LOSE BEFORE YOU LOSE TOO MUCH AND HAVE RECONSIDER YOUR GOALS.

The core equation that I use to determine her portfolio's value along the way is a variation of a loan payment formula:

$$P(1 + r)^n + [(M/n)((1 + r)^n - 1)]$$

where:

P = Start Amount

r = Portfolio Return (decimal) divided by 12

n = Timeframe in years x 12

M = Monthly Contribution

Don't panic – I'll show you how to use it. It's easier than it seems.

Using the equation, I figured out that at the end of 6 years, Ivana has $646,897.

She subsequently changes her portfolio to target a 6% return, invests for another 3 years, and ends up with $793,797.

Ivana wants to retire with $750,000, and her estimated end portfolio value is $793,797. She currently may have a surplus of $43,797.

Here are the inputs to the equation:

First 6 years:

P = $350,000 starting amount

r = .09/12 = .0075 portfolio return per month

n = 6 years x 12 = 72 months

M = $500 contributed per month

Her portfolio value at the end of the first 6 years is $561,269.

Last 3 years:

P = $646,897 starting amount

r = .06/12 = .005 portfolio return per month

n = 3 x 12 = 36 months

M = $500 contributed per month

Her portfolio value at the end of the following 3 years is $793,797.

WORKBOOK GUIDE: GO TO THE "MANAGING LOSSES" TAB. IT HAS IVANA RETIRE'S EXAMPLE PREFILLED.

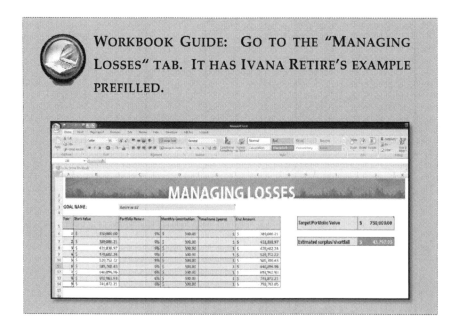

As discussed earlier, the market does not move in a straight line. Some years, you may have an actual return less than your average annual target. And some years, you may have a return much larger than your target.

Knowing this, Ivana decided to check how much a bad year in the stock market would affect her future plans. The workbook will once again make your life much easier in this step. It already has Ivana's example prefilled, broken down by year.

Ivana put together a portfolio on her "My Portfolios" tab that she expects to give her a 9% average annual return. Before she invests, she tested what would happen if the market had a terrible year during her first year of investing, and her portfolio ended the year with a -5% return.

She put -5% in the Portfolio Return cell for her first year, and saw immediately that she may have a $50,495 shortfall:

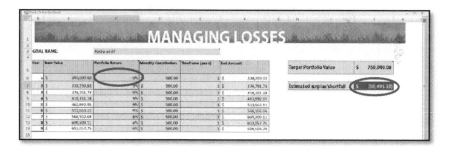

She played with her portfolio return in the workbook for Year 2, and saw that she may need a 17% return in Year 2 to get back on track! Alternatively, 13% returns in Years 2 and 3 may work as well.

Looking at the stocks in her portfolio under "My Portfolio", the maximum average annual return that any of her stocks had was 38% (coincidentally, Apple!).

	Ticker	Market Capitalization	Beta	Industry	Sector	Country	Last Close Price	Avg. Annual Return	Shares	Portfolio Value	Weight	Weighted Return
6	AAPL	Mega Cap	1.23	Technology	Computer Hardware	US	$ 631.09	38.80%	75	$47,326.75	14%	5.52%
7	GOOG	Mega Cap	1.06	Technology	Computer Services	US	$ 668.66	5.62%	50	$33,433.00	10%	0.57%
8	TGT	Large Cap	0.37	Retail (Specialty)	Services	US	$ 63.38	2.45%	750	$47,535.00	14%	0.35%
9	JNJ	Large Cap	1.04	Aerospace and Defense	Capital Goods	US	$ 68.64	5.19%	1500	$102,960.00	31%	1.61%
10	PG	Large Cap	0.45	Personal and Household	Consumer/Non-Cyclical	US	$ 66.73	3.37%	1500	$100,095.00	30%	1.08%
11	**Total Portfolio Value**			$331,399.75						Estimated Avg Annual Portfolio Return:		9.13%

She could "rebalance" or adjust her share amounts to have a greater proportion of high-returning stocks. However, that would cause her portfolio to have an uncomfortable level of risk.

While an overall return of 17% may be possible if the market surges back, Ivana plans to sell before her portfolio dips 5% in any year. She doesn't have time in the market to recover.

Ivana checks the "YTD return" (e.g., "year to date return") of each of her stocks every 3 months (e.g., every quarter).

On each stock's Google Finance homepage, she clicks "YTD" in the chart area and gets the YTD return in parentheses at the top of the chart. In this snapshot on the next page, we see that Proctor and Gamble has a YTD return of -.19%:

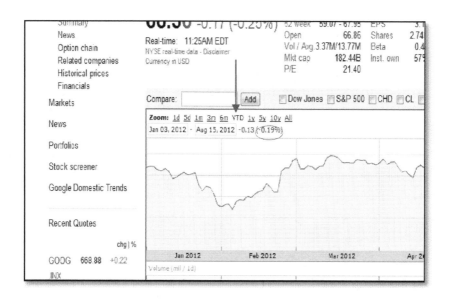

Ivana uses this to compare to the "Avg. Annual Return" values that she used when she put together her portfolio on the "My Portfolios" tab:

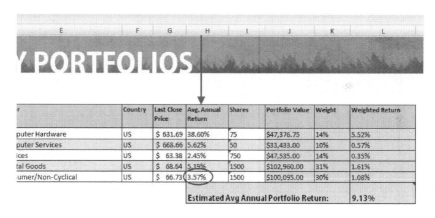

r	Country	Last Close Price	Avg. Annual Return	Shares	Portfolio Value	Weight	Weighted Return
puter Hardware	US	$ 631.69	38.60%	75	$47,376.75	14%	5.52%
puter Services	US	$ 668.66	5.62%	50	$33,433.00	10%	0.57%
ices	US	$ 63.38	2.45%	750	$47,535.00	14%	0.35%
tal Goods	US	$ 68.64	5.19%	1500	$102,960.00	31%	1.61%
umer/Non-Cyclical	US	$ 66.73	3.57%	1500	$100,095.00	30%	1.08%
			Estimated Avg Annual Portfolio Return:				9.13%

In this example, Proctor and Gamble has a YTD return of -.19% from the chart. Ivana used 3.57% in her estimate.

She replaced 3.57% with -.19%, and saw that her overall portfolio return would be approximately 8%.

Ivana wondered if an 8% return during her first year would cause her to miss her target.

She put 8% into the Portfolio Return cell for Year 1 on the "Managing Losses" tab, and saw that she still may be able to hit her target, and even have a surplus:

Her estimated surplus, however, would drop from $43,797 to $36,656.

After further tweaking, she realized that she would need at least a 3% return in Year 1 in order to hit her target portfolio value. With this in mind, she checks in on her portfolio on a quarterly basis, and if necessary she rebalances or changes how she allocates her monthly contribution.

She does not have to worry about paying capital gains taxes in an IRA. Nevertheless, speak with a tax advisor to understand how rebalancing your portfolio affects your personal situation.

Advanced Techniques to Limit Portfolio Losses

Although this is a book about buying stocks online, I did want to cover advanced techniques to limit losses in your stock portfolio. Please feel free to skip this section if your head already hurts!

Shorting Against the Box

When investors short a stock, they sell a stock that they do not own. They'll subsequently buy shares later to close out the short position. The profit comes when you buy back the stock at a lower price than what you sold it.

As long as the price continues to fall, the investor will make a profit on a short position.

If the investor closes the position by buying stock, the difference between the sell price and purchase price is the investor's profit.

If the price of a shorted stock goes up past the original "sell" price, the investor will lose money. In theory, losses can be unlimited since a stock price can go to infinity. So shorting is an advanced technique to do by itself.

However, if you combine a short position with a preexisting position (e.g., a "long" position), your broker may allow you close out your short position with your preexisting long shares. This is called "Shorting Against the Box".

If your long position starts to decline, and if you short that stock, you lock in your gain or loss on the long position. You can use this same technique to lock in a gain to delay selling and paying capital gains taxes.

While both long and short positions are open, you lock in whatever profit or loss you had on your long position until you "flatten" your long and short shares to close out your short position.

Keep in mind that you can also buy stock to close out the short position, leaving your original long position intact. Alternatively, you can sell your original long position and leave your short position intact.

Also keep in mind that there are tax and cost basis implications for attempting to lock in short-term gains towards converting to long-term gains. Please discuss these with a tax advisor.

A bit of trivia – "shorting against the box" got its name because your original long shares are theoretically in a "lockbox" and not being used immediately to close out your new short position.

Buying Put Options

Buying a put option will give you the right (but not the obligation) to sell your stock at a particular price in the future.

It allows you to protect your position so that you have the flexibility to sell it in the future at a higher price if that's what you choose to do.

The future price in the put option contract is the "strike" price. Ideally, you'd buy a put option with a higher strike price than your existing position's cost basis.

You may ask why don't all investors buy put options to protect their profits? Because buying put options costs money, and put options expire.

As a result, it's typically a one-time strategy that's used when an investor faces losing money on a position yet doesn't want to sell the position yet. It is not typically used as an ongoing protection strategy since it costs money.

Covered Calls

Buying a call option gives an investor the right to buy stock at a particular price in the future. But what if you don't want to buy stock, but just protect your existing position so that you may be able to sell it at a particular price in the future?

Using the "covered call" technique means you are *selling* call options to another investor. As a result, the other investor may choose to buy your stock at a specific price in the future.

This may sound similar to a put option. Covered calls, however, involves your selling options on your existing positions. As a result, you make money each time you sell a call options contract.

Unfortunately, the buyer of the call option has the right to buy your stock at the option's strike price. As a result, you will be forced to sell your stock when another investor exercises their call options contract.

Key Takeaways

✓ Before you buy a stock, understand how much you would be willing to watch that stock decline before you exit or cover the position.

✓ When a stock position loses money, the position has to recover its losses before the position becomes profitable again. The length of time a stock takes to recover its losses could potentially make you lose progress towards meeting your goal amount within your timeframe.

✓ Use the workbook to determine how much your portfolio can stand to lose before you're not able to hit your target portfolio value.

✓ An investor has several tools in his or her toolbox to keep a portfolio from bleeding losses. Those tools include rebalancing, selling a losing position, buying an uncorrelated stock, shorting against the box, covered calls, and buying put options.

Remember than the workbook only provides an estimate. It is not recommended to use it as a sole guide to determine whether you buy or sell stocks. Please speak with an experienced professional that you know and trust to determine the right course of action for your situation.

STEP 7 : CHOOSE AN ONLINE DISCOUNT BROKER AND SIGN UP!

Picking an online broker these days is like going on reality dating show and choosing a partner.

Perhaps you like Joe because he's sophisticated, or Jeff because he's handy.

Perhaps you just like the way John looks, and you don't care that he doesn't do much else besides look good.

The great part about today's selection of online brokers is that there is something for everyone. And the bad part? There is something for everyone.

By my last count, there are over 25 different choices for online brokers! I won't even try to rank them all. It might make your head spin!

In fact, if you search online for "Online Broker Comparison", you will surely find reviews of all available brokers at hundreds of websites.

So instead of reviewing every single broker, I'll give you the names of ones with which I have personal experience and liked. Subsequently, please perform your own due diligence to find the best online broker for your specific situation.

 SEARCHING FOR AN ONLINE BROKER CAN MAKE YOUR HEAD SPIN! USE THE FOLLOWING CRITERIA AND SUGGESTIONS TO NARROW DOWN YOUR SEARCH.

Online Broker Criteria

When I've picked an online broker in the past for either myself or someone else, I used the following five pieces of criteria:

1. Integration/Export Capabilities

One broker will not have all of the tools that you need to manage your portfolio. As a result, you may want to manage your portfolio in an accounting program like QuickBooks, Google Finance, or even into your Modern Wealth Media workbook!

Check if the broker allows you to download (e.g., "export") your transactions to a file so that you can import your transactions into another application.

Example export formats include CSV, XLS, PDX, IIF, and OFX.

If you use financial software, check the "import formats" that they accept. Then, check that your broker of choice *exports* into that format.

Alternatively, your software may directly connect to online brokers. Mint.com – a popular personal finance application – allows users to set up a direct connection to a number of discount brokers. Therefore, check if your software can connect to the broker of your choice before opening an account.

Finally, check that your online broker of choice accepts electronic funds transfers (e.g. ACH or Wire transfers) to and from your bank. Most do, but it doesn't hurt to double check.

2. <u>Risk and Return Monitoring</u>

I may be a risk and return geek, but I highly recommend monitoring these two things on an ongoing basis. A broker that provides tools to support you earns a checkmark in my book.

Their tools should allow you to monitor risk and return at the stock level, and the portfolio level. Check if you can see stock and portfolio level beta and standard deviation. Can you also compare your portfolio's historical performance to any global benchmark?

Also, check if the broker has charting tools to compare your "principal" amount to your "portfolio value". This will help you visually see your profit:

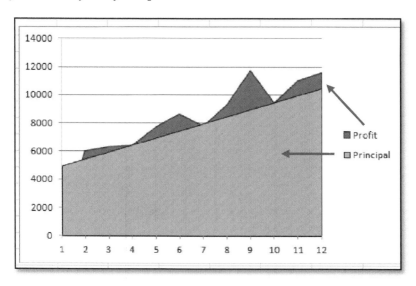

It's a plus if you can check your portfolio's country, sector and industry exposures – e.g., what percentage of your portfolio has US stocks, what percentage of your portfolio has technology investments, etc. This may go by the name of a "Portfolio X-Ray".

Not many online brokers provide all of these capabilities. But ones that do get a gold star from me.

3. Trading

Discount brokers should actually provide you with a discount! So if their commissions are more than $9 per stock trade, I would look elsewhere.

An online broker may charge extra for "lightly traded" stocks. These stocks trade with a low volume, and are on their way up (e.g., startups) or on their way down (e.g., delisted from major exchanges). Examples of these include penny stocks that trade on the Pink Sheets or Over-the-Counter Bulletin Board systems.

An online broker may also charge extra for "broker assisted" trades. For example, an online broker may force you to call a live broker to place a penny stock order, or an order for a large trade.

Both surcharges are normal – nevertheless, check the fees.

If you are planning to contribute to your account each month, check if a broker provides an Automatic Investment Plan. You may be able to get discounted commissions if you participate.

Although we've been discussing buying stocks online, check that your online broker also allows other asset classes. This includes bonds, mutual funds, ETFs, UITs, and Options. Bonds, ETFs, and mutual funds should be sufficient if you are a new investor. Note that "bonds" includes treasuries and CD's.

In this day and age, an online broker should provide you with free real-time quotes. When you decide to buy or sell, you'll make that decision while viewing the most recent market price with real time quotes. As a side note, free sites like Google Finance show quotes delayed by at least 15-20 minutes.

Finally, it's a plus if the online broker provides "virtual" or "paper" trading. This enables you to build and manage a portfolio without placing real trades. As a result, you can test your skills without using any of your money!

One more thing: it's an even bigger plus if the broker allows you to give each account a "nickname". This will allow you to use each purpose as the nickname on each account. You'll subsequently never forget why you're investing.

4. Research/Reporting

Wouldn't it help you tremendously to perform your stock research directly at your online broker's website?

Whether it's the broker's in-house research or whether they provide research from another provider like Morningstar, having access to research at your broker's site may make your life easier.

Knowing what you need

to manage your portfolio and find stocks

will help you find an online broker

that best fulfills your needs.

Be careful, however, to use research from a reputable company. A quick online search may help you gauge a company's reputation.

If your broker of choice offers more than one asset class, ensure that the research also covers those other asset classes.

For example, can you see into the broker's bond inventory, and can you research bond rates? Does the broker provide mutual fund research on a comprehensive universe of mutual funds (typically more than 1700 mutual funds)?

Finally, it's a plus if you can export a performance or gain/loss report on your portfolio for your records (or for your tax advisor).

5. Overall User Experience

With over 25 online brokers available and counting, you can surely find a site with the look, feel, and functionality you need.

Is the site intuitive? Can you click around the site and not get lost or confused? Does the site make you feel welcome, or intimidated?

For more advanced investors, how quickly can you jump to the tools that you need? Does the site have distracting elements like ads (hopefully not)? Does the site have a dashboard that gives you a bird's eye view of the market and your portfolio?

Also, does the broker have account minimums? If you're a beginner, try to avoid a broker that has a minimum. This will allow you to sign up for an account and test drive the site before you transfer money.

How easily can you open additional accounts? It's a plus if you can link your accounts together and transfer money between them – in particular, for accounts within a family.

Finally, how easily can you get in touch with a live customer support representative? It's a plus if one calls you after you open an account – a personal touch that is rare in the discount broker world!

Online Broker Recommendations

What follows are my top three recommendations based upon my personal experience. This isn't an exhaustive review or commentary of all available online brokers. Also, I'm not compensated for any of these reviews.

I ranked each by experience level, so hopefully that will guide you towards finding the most suitable site. Keep in mind that you can transfer your account to another broker at any time.

Nevertheless, please perform your own due diligence before you open an account.

SEARCH FOR BROKER REVIEWS FROM REPUTABLE ONLINE SOURCES AND TALK WITH SOMEONE THAT YOU KNOW AND TRUST TO FIND THE ONLINE BROKER THAT BEST FULFILLS YOUR NEEDS.

For Beginners: ShareBuilder.com

It takes less than 10 minutes to open an account at Sharebuilder, which speaks to the intuitiveness of their site. It's a very stripped down site. It primarily has the essentials that a beginner needs. As a result, you're less likely to get confused or intimidated.

Sharebuilder doesn't have an account minimum. This may be its biggest plus. You can open a free account and look around before you transfer money.

Sharebuilder only has stocks, ETFs, mutual funds and options – e.g., no bonds, CDs, and other fixed income products. However, Sharebuilder's parent company is ING. As a result, you have access to ING's high-yield money market funds, which provides some of the best rates in the industry.

Overall, it's a basic site with bread and butter tools for new investors who don't plan on trading often.

For Intermediate Investors: Zecco.com (merging with TradeKing.com)

Zecco also takes less than 10 minutes to open an account. They have a slick, intuitive interface plus highly rated mobile tools. They also offer real-time streaming quotes for free!

Zecco also doesn't have an account minimum. As a result, you can create an account and look around to see if Zecco is right for you.

You can buy stocks, ETFs, options, mutual funds, currencies (e.g., Foreign Exchange or FOREX), and bonds at Zecco. Their stock commissions are very low (currently $4.95/trade).

Zecco has a solid online community where you can ask questions to experienced traders and investors. This is a plus as you are growing and refining your skills.

Zecco isn't perfect – for example, I've heard mixed reviews about their customer service. However, it is certainly worth your time to investigate it.

For Advanced Investors: Scottrade.com

Scottrade has a high degree of customization and flexibility. You can design your own dashboard using a number of widgets, which I love.

Scottrade integrated Morningstar's research into its platform. You can easily access high quality research reports from within your account. This research, combined with its screeners and comparison tools, helps in finding investment opportunities quickly.

Even if you are a new investor, yet comfortable working online, Scottrade may work for you.

Scottrade simply has a comprehensive platform. Nevertheless, each advanced investor has his or her preferences and quirks. Platforms that are much more powerful exist for professionals (like Bloomberg, of course!). Many financial professionals have accounts where their work for compliance reasons anyway, and don't typically use discount brokers.

Nevertheless, if trading is not your day job yet you have experience as an investor, you may find a home at Scottrade.

Key Takeaways

✓ An abundance of online brokers exists. Each has features for every kind of investor.

✓ Catalogue your needs, and use that as a guide to find the broker that suits you best.

✓ You are responsible for evaluating the benefits and risks associated with using an online broker. You are also responsible for deciding which securities and strategies best suit your financial situation, goals and risk profile.

Please speak with a professional that you know and trust before you trade.

STEP 8: PLACE YOUR TRADES

Congratulations on taking another step into the world of online trading! In this step, we're focusing on how to place a trade with an online discount broker.

Before you start placing trades, I highly recommend kicking the tires at the brokerage site that you chose. Take a tutorial, dig into sample reports, "paper trade", or compile a list of questions for customer service.

Please make sure you are comfortable with the site before you unpack your suitcase, and place your trades. While you can easily transfer your account from one broker to another, save yourself the hassle of completing transfer paperwork by making sure you are happy with the broker that you chose.

Each online broker has a different layout to the screen where you place your orders – e.g., the "trade entry" or "order entry" screen. However, common requirements exist between all trade entry screens, including entering:

➢ Your Action (e.g., buying or selling)
➢ Your Symbol
➢ Number of Shares
➢ Order Type

Let's step through each requirement, using ShareBuilder as an example.

Once again, while your order entry screen may look different, many of the core elements may be the same.

How to Enter an Order

1. Action

Here is where you indicate your intention for placing an order –
e.g., to buy shares, or to sell shares.

You may have additional options, including:

➢ Buy to Cover: Buying stocks to cover/close an existing short
  position

➢ Sell Short: Opening a short position (note that you need to have "margin" privileges on your account, per regulations. Margin allows you to borrow cash from your online broker using the cash and securities in your account as collateral.)

➢ Sell Short Exempt: Opening a short position that is exempt from the "uptick rule". This rule prevents short trades from executing until the next time the market price ticks up. This prevents short orders from pushing the market downward due to selling pressure. This option only applies in special trading situations.

2. Symbol
The two-four character symbol for the stock that you wish to trade.

Most order entry screens will also show you the latest market price for your symbol. Note that if you're buying, your trade will execute at the stock's "ask" price. If you're selling, your trade will execute at the stock's "bid" price.

Please keep in mind that the price you see quoted may or may not be the latest real-time quote for your stock.

As a result, your order may ultimately execute at a price greater than or less than what you see in the order entry screen.

3. Number of Shares

How many shares you want to buy or sell.

You may have a "Share Calculator" that will allow you to figure out the cost of your trade, including commissions.

Sites like Sharebuilder will even show you the maximum number of shares that you can purchase with the cash in your account.

Alternatively, your broker may ask you to provide a dollar amount instead of a share amount, which I prefer. Subsequently, the broker will buy as many shares as possible for your dollar amount, including commissions.

4. Order Type

Several types of orders are possible, including:

➢ Market Order: Nine times out of ten, you will need to place this type of order. This tells the online broker to execute your order at the most current "ask" price if you are buying, or "bid" price if you are selling.

If the market is closed, your trade will execute at the start of the next business day. In the US, the market opens at 9:30 AM EST, and closes at 4 PM EST.

Your market order may execute at an unexpected bid or ask price. To control the price at which you're buying or selling, use one of the following two order types.

➤ Limit Order: When you select the option to place a limit order, the order entry screen may change to allow you to enter a "limit price".

Together, your limit order instruction and your limit price tell your broker one of two things.

If you're buying shares, these instructions tell your broker to execute your buy order at or *below* the price that you gave.

If you're selling shares, these instructions tell your broker to execute your order at or *above* the price that you gave.

Limit orders protect you from having your order execute at a market price that is *worse* than you intended. You would place it below the current market price if you're buying, or above the current market price if you're selling.

Please read your broker's fine print about fees and timing if only part of your order could be executed at the price that you gave (e.g., "partially filled orders").

Note that you are only guaranteed a fill if the market price passes *through* your limit price (not close to or exactly at), and if your broker can find a market maker/et al with the inventory (e.g., liquidity or volume) to complete your trade.

➤ Stop/Loss Order: As the name implies, use this to place orders that may prevent losses in your portfolio.

For example, you may have an existing position that you want to sell if the price falls to a certain level. Enter a sell stop/loss at that price level to trigger the sell when the market price reaches that level.

On the flip side, you may have an open short position that you want to cover if the price rises to a certain level. A buy stop/loss would do the trick.

Once again, your order entry screen may change to allow you to enter a price if you select "Stop/Loss" as your order type. When the market price passes through your stop order price, it will execute if the volume facilitates it.

Read your online broker's documentation carefully to determine the best order for your needs.

5. Time in Force

Although you don't see this on the Sharebuilder order entry screen snapshot, you may have the option to tell the broker how long to keep your order active.

Don't forget that in certain cases, your order can't be executed right way. If you have a limit or stop/loss order, or if you're trading a stock that has a low trading volume, your order may take time to trigger or fill.

Three typical "time in force" instructions include:

➤ Day Order: This tells your broker to cancel your order if it did not execute by the time the market closes for the day.

➤ Good Till Canceled: This tells your broker to keep your order open until you cancel it, even if it doesn't execute by the time the market closes.

➤ All or None: This tells your broker to either completely fill your order at the same price, or cancel it.

➤ Fill or Kill: This tells your broker to fill your entire order completely and immediately, or cancel your order. "Immediate or Cancel" is similar – however, Immediate or Cancel allows for partial fills, and only the unfilled part of the order will be cancelled.

Whew! That's a long list of things to consider as you're placing a trade. Most of the time, however, you will simply place a Buy or Sell, Good Till Canceled Market Order. So do not lose sleep if you don't understand the other types of instructions just yet.

As you become more experienced, you will naturally check how a limit or stop/loss order may help you in managing your profits and losses.

Nevertheless, carefully review your broker's available order instructions. Most importantly, ensure you understand the fees involved with your trades prior to entering an order.

And if you're still nervous, please "paper trade" if your online broker allows it. You can practice entering orders without the threat of making a mistake.

If you do make a mistake, call your broker immediately to try to attempt to cancel your order.

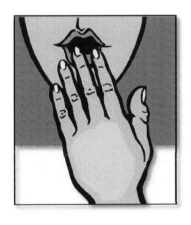

IF YOU MAKE A MISTAKE WHILE ENTERING AN ORDER, CALL CUSTOMER SERVICE IMMEDIATELY! DO NOT TRADE UNTIL YOU'RE COMFORTABLE PLACING ORDERS.

Key Takeaways

✓ Depending on your online broker, your order entry screen
   may have different types of instructions.

   Common instructions on all order screens include:

   ➢ Action: Buy or Sell
   ➢ Symbol: Know your two to four-character stock symbol
   ➢ Number of Shares/Even Dollar Amount: How many
      shares you want to buy, or the maximum amount of
      money that you want to spend.
   ➢ Type of Order: Market, Limit, or Stop/Loss
   ➢ Time in Force: Good Till Canceled, Day Order, Fill or
      Kill, All or None

✓ Don't forget to factor in commissions when you plan your
   order. Most online brokers will help you with this
   calculation directly in the order screen.

✓ Ensure you understand your broker's fees before you place a
   trade.

STEP 9: MONITOR AND KNOW WHEN TO TAKE ACTION

You're in the home stretch!! You checked your budget, did your research, constructed a portfolio, and bought stocks at an online broker.

And that wasn't even the hard part.

The hard part is controlling the fear that will swell in your gut whenever you hear news that may affect your portfolio.

Surely, this doesn't apply to you. You're now a cool-headed investor who knows exactly how much you can lose, and how to get yourself back on track.

Nevertheless, we're all human. So take action before you panic, and use the following tools to gain an understanding of what's happening in the market before getting the uncontrollable urge to hit the sell button.

BAD NEWS MAY MAKE YOU WANT TO SELL, SELL, SELL! PREPARE YOURSELF BY SETTING UP TOOLS TO MONITOR YOUR PORTFOLIO, AND BY HAVING AN MARKET EXIT STRATEGY.

Monitor News Related to Your Portfolio

When you monitor news, you're looking for events that may cause the long-term value of a company to change.

Examples include if a company increases dividends, or releases a successful new product. After you do a fundamental analysis the first time (such as what we completed in Step 4 for Target), you will understand the factors that could influence a stock's price.

Your online broker of choice likely provides a feed with news stories related to the stocks in your portfolio. You can also go onto the Reuters website and scan the "Key Developments" on your stock's "homepage" at least quarterly:

Google Finance has an excellent free interface for you to monitor news related to stocks in your portfolio. To do this, you have to set up a portfolio in Google Finance. Google will then show you news stories related to the stocks in your Google portfolio automatically.

Setting up a portfolio in Google Finance does not mean that you're actually trading. It's just a watchlist. No money is involved.

How to Setup a Portfolio in Google Finance:

➢ Go to http://finance.google.com.
➢ Click on "Portfolios" in the left hand side menu. You'll be taken to another page.
➢ Click "Create new portfolio" in the upper right hand corner of the page. I recommend using the name of each purpose as the portfolio name (for example, "Buy a Home").
➢ Add symbols to the portfolio. In my sample portfolio, I'm adding Apple and Google to my portfolio:

➢ Next, if you are able to export transactions from your online broker, do so in CSV or OFX format so that you can import them into your Google portfolio.

Otherwise, click the "Edit transactions" link above the table. Enter your "cost basis" information – including the date that you purchased shares, the quantity, the price, and the commission charged.

Note that you don't have to enter transaction information if you don't want to monitor your unrealized gains and losses. Your gains and losses are "unrealized" until you close/exit your positions. Then, your gains and losses become "realized".

Once you add stocks to a Google portfolio, the bottom half of the screen will show "Portfolio related news" – e.g., news stories that mention the companies in your Google portfolio:

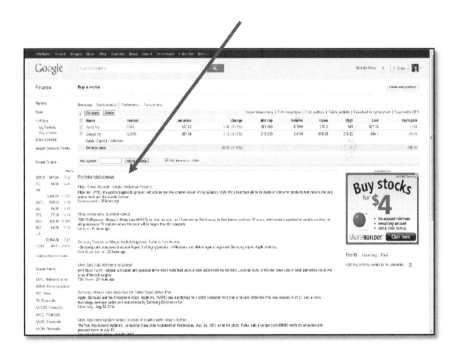

This is a quick and easy way to stay on top of related news stories.

Keep in mind certain news stories may cause a temporary panic – for example, if a bad PR event happens such as a product recall or CEO firings.

As a result, you will constantly need to use your judgment to determine whether a story will fundamentally change the value of a company or not. That judgment gets refined each time you complete a fundamental analysis. So while the research process can be painful and intricate, it helps you as an investor.

Monitor Benchmarks That Match Your Portfolio

A quick way to stay on top of your portfolio's performance is to keep an eye on a benchmark (e.g., an index) that mirrors the composition of your portfolio.

If you buy stocks from companies whose products you like, your portfolio will likely have stocks from the country in which you live. You can double check this by reviewing the country that you documented on the "My Portfolios" tab.

You should have documented the Market Capitalization, sector, and industry on that sheet as well:

If you have a column where the majority of your stocks have the same value, use that as part of your criteria for finding a relevant index.

For example, the majority of the stocks in the portfolio above are Large Cap US companies. As a result, any changes in the Large Cap US market may hint at similar changes happening in my portfolio.

You can even watch sector and industry indices if those have relevance to your stock picks.

To find the index that best matches your portfolio's market capitalization and country, start by observing which indices the news always mentions.

For example, the US media consistently reports changes in the S&P and Dow indices. In Europe, the FTSE, DAC, and CAC are popular. In Asia, reporters consistently mention the Nikkei and Hang Seng indices.

*Monitoring an **index** is a quick way to keep an eye on factors that may **impact** your portfolio.*

Next, use a search engine to search for a list of indices under the appropriate country. For example, since most of my stocks are in the US, I would search for "S&P indices" or "Dow indices".

Subsequently, you should be able to find an appropriate benchmark on the firm's website. For example, Standard and Poors (e.g., S&P) describes what's in each benchmark so that you can match it against the majority composition of your portfolio.

Nine times out of ten, the index or indices mentioned most in the news should work for you.

Perform an Annual Research Checkup

On a yearly basis, check up on your stocks' outlook by redoing the 10-step research process for the stocks in your portfolio.

If you stayed current on news stories related to your stocks, this checkup should be a quick process. You're primarily looking for changes that will impact the value of the stock.

It's possible that a stock's role in your portfolio may change. For example, Apple was once an aggressive Small Cap startup. Now, it's a stately Mega Cap.

Stay on top of changes so that you don't end up with a stock that no longer supports your investment objectives.

Check the Winners and Losers

On an annual basis, it's a good idea to check which stocks in your portfolio contribute the least to your overall portfolio return.

On the "My Portfolio" workbook, you made a record of each stock's historical average portfolio return. You may have used these returns as a guide in building your portfolio, and estimating its overall historical average return.

If a stock has been having poor performance relative to its past returns, it may be a signal that its fundamentals have changed. After you perform a checkup, you may decide that it's time to either reduce your shares in that stock, or sell completely.

On the flip side, if a stock has been having outstanding performance, that stock may have become "overweight" in your portfolio. It may make up a greater share of your portfolio value than you previously planned for it to have.

Use your discretion going forward. You can sell some of your shares and buy more of the other stocks in your portfolio (e.g., perform a "rebalance"), or just focus your monthly contribution into buying other stocks in your portfolio.

Before you take action, ensure that you're aware of any tax consequences with buying or selling by discussing the proper course of action for your situation with an advisor.

Jensen's Alpha

And now for something a bit more advanced.

Nearly every letter of the Greek alphabet has a use in finance –alpha, beta, gamma, sigma, and so on.

Finding your portfolio's "Jensen's Alpha" can tell you how great of job you did in picking stocks. Or not.

Economist Michael C. Jensen developed this metric in 1968 as a way to compare the performance of mutual fund managers. Since stock-based mutual funds are just portfolios of stocks, this metric should also be usable by individual investors to rate their own performance in picking stocks for their portfolio.

Let's take the following portfolio as an example: Proctor and Gamble, United Technologies, Apple and Goldman Sachs.

Let's assume that after checking my average annual portfolio return in Google portfolios or on my brokerage site, and I saw that it was 9.5%.

Also, assume that the S&P 500 best reflects the types of stocks I chose for my portfolio. So I've chosen that as my benchmark.

If during that same period the S&P 500 returned 10%, did I outperform the market?

It seems like I didn't. My portfolio returned less than the S&P 500. However, did I make my return with less risk than the S&P 500?

For comparison, if I piloted a plane from New York to California in 6 hours, and if you drove the same distance in 2 days, who performed better?

In the Modern Portfolio Theory world, you performed better. I'm not a professional pilot. Nevertheless, I arrived in California in just 6 hours. That's expected for a plane trip from New York. Plus, I took more risk to make my trip because, after all, I'm not a professional pilot.

You took far less risk by driving. You also got to California from New York in far less time than anyone would have expected (2 days instead of the typical 4 days). As a result, you performed much better than I did because you outperformed expectations given the amount of risk that you took.

Jensen's Alpha works the same way. This metric compares the "risk adjusted" actual return of your portfolio to a return that represents the overall market for your portfolio. In other words, this metric factors in the amount of risk you took (or didn't take) into your overall performance. It also quantifies how well you picked stocks.

The more positive this number is, the better than expected your portfolio is performing and the more you are theoretically beating the market.

How to Use Jenson's Alpha

The formula for Jensen's Alpha is:

Jensen's Alpha = Actual Return ⁻ Market Return

where:

Actual Return = Your portfolio's actual average annual return

Market Return = Return of the market that best mirrors your stock selection

Your online broker should have analysis tools to help you determine your portfolio's average annual return. If not, you can estimate it by using the Modern Wealth Media workbook's "My Portfolios" tab. It should already be calculated for you if you completed the table for your portfolio in Chapter/Step 5.

The formula to find out the Market Return is:

Risk Free Rate of Return + Portfolio Beta x (Benchmark Return ⁻ Risk Free Rate of Return)

Formula geeks may recognize this as the Capital Asset Pricing Model.

The "Risk Free Rate of Return" represents the interest rate for an investment that has zero risk of principal loss or default.

There are different schools of thought as to which rate to use as the risk free rate. Nevertheless, in the US, the annual interest rate for a 3-month US Treasury Bill is typically used. Today in 2012, that rate is .06% – extremely low.

You can find this by going to http://finance.yahoo.com/bonds. Believe it or not, it was as high as 5% in 2007.

Next, you can estimate your portfolio's beta by either using tools at your online broker, or by using the Modern Wealth Media "My Portfolios" tab. It's a weighted sum of each stock's beta.

Finally, check the average annual return for the benchmark that you chose in the "Monitor Benchmarks That Match Your Portfolio" section of this chapter. You should find this by visiting the website of the company that maintains the index.

Try to match the timeframe to the timeframe for the stock returns used in your portfolio. For example, in Step 5 in the "Build Your Portfolio" section, you looked up average annual returns for each stock in your portfolio on Morningstar. If you picked 5-Yr average annual returns for each stock in your portfolio, use the 5-Yr average annual return for your chosen benchmark here.

Let's put this all together for a sample portfolio using the S&P 500 as a benchmark.

Note that I used 5-Yr TR (Total Return) average annual returns from Morningstar for each stock in my portfolio in the workbook (see below). As a result, I will use the 5-Yr TR average annual return for the S&P 500. Today, that value is 1.13%. "Total Return" includes dividends, capital gains, and distributions.

On the surface, it appears that my portfolio (which has an estimated 5-Yr average annual return of 9.13%) is outperforming the S&P 500.

Example (Jensen's Alpha)

Sample Portfolio (prefilled in the Modern Wealth Media workbook):

Jensen's Alpha = Actual Return - Market Return

Actual Return = 9.13%

Market Return =

Risk Free Rate of Return + Portfolio Beta x (Benchmark Return - Risk Free Rate of Return)

$$= .06\% + .87 \times (1.13\% - .06\%) = .99\%$$

Jensen's Alpha = 9.13% - .99% = 8.14%!

That's a great big positive number! This number would have obviously been different if we used a different risk free rate. Also, Jensen's Alpha is more useful when you compare it to the Jensen's Alpha for another portfolio.

Nevertheless, in this example, the positive value means that we did a great job in picking stocks. Which shouldn't come as a surprise – Apple had a 38% average annual return over the previous 5 years, and is a part of this portfolio.

Alternatives to Jensen's Alpha exist, such as a performance attribution analysis which actually helps you pinpoint the investment or allocation choices that you made to cause the under- or outperformance.

But if you thought that Jensen's Alpha was overkill, explaining how to do a performance attribution analysis is definitely too much information – especially if your portfolio only has a handful of stocks. As a result, it's out of scope for this book. But I wouldn't rule this out as a blog entry.

If You're Still Thinking About Changing Your Portfolio...

Speak with a professional that you know and trust – in particular, regarding any tax implications.

Additional Ways to Monitor Performance

Monitoring performance can feel like drinking from a firehose. Not only are you processing news and fundamental data changes in your portfolio, but you also are monitoring the overall market for your portfolio by watching a benchmark.

Don't cause information overload. Everyday investors generally just need to watch headlines, perform a checkup each quarter, and a comprehensive review annually.

Nevertheless, other sources besides the ones previously mentioned may help you keep on top of changes as they happen.

Financial News

If you're a news hound, watching a station like Bloomberg may help expose you to additional ways of interpreting trends and indicators. It's also an excellent way to stay on top of "macro" level news affecting the broader economy, such as Federal Reserve announcements. You can find Bloomberg on cable, or online at http://www.bloomberg.com/tv.

I really love Bloomberg. However, you may find that other stations such as CNBC fit your needs. Perhaps you don't need to watch a 24 financial news network, and reading a paper such as the Financial Times works for you (another one of my favorites).

Other Types of Indices

Benchmarks have company. Other types indices exist to help you take the temperature of the overall market.

For example, the St. Louis Federal Reserve created the "Financial Stress Index" in the early 1990's to quantify the "flight to safety" in the overall market. "Flight to safety" happens when investors sell off risky assets like stocks, and buy assets where their principal is "safer" like Treasuries.

In the past, this index has tended to spike during a recession – in particular, when the financial system crashed in 2008:

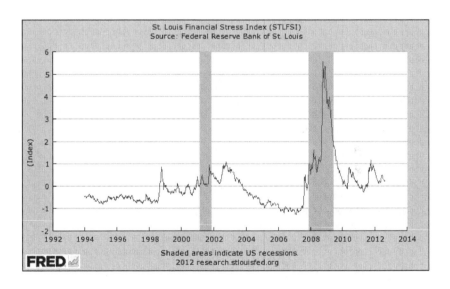

You can find this chart at http://research.stlousifed.org.

Yet another index tends to spike when trouble is brewing in the markets: the Chicago Board Options Exchange's Volatility Index (also known as the "VIX").

Investors also refer to this index as the "fear gauge". In other words, markets tend to become volatile when fear increases.

This index gauges fear by using S&P 500 index options. You can find this at Yahoo! finance under the symbol "^VIX":

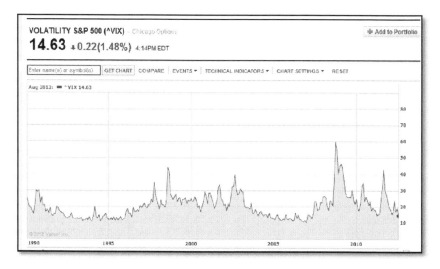

Economic Indicators

Economic indicators help in tracking the health of an overall economy. Leading economic indicators in particular can help investors preview whether an economy may improve or not before it actually starts to happen. Nearly every country publishes economic indicators.

While individual indicators can be useful to track (such as Consumer Confidence and Employment indicators), the

Conference Board Leading Economic Index® aggregates 10 key leading economic indicators into one. They do this for 11 countries.

If you go to http://www.conference-board.org and click on the collapsible menu for "Global Indicators" under "Economic Indicators" on the upper right hand side, you'll see the latest update for each index:

Clicking on each country name will give you the board's analysis of changes in the index. It's a nice tool for getting a big picture, "macro" understanding for how global economies are trending.

Key Takeaways

✓ Monitoring related news, indices, and portfolio performance can be one of the most psychologically trying parts of buying stocks online.

✓ As a long-term investor, perform quarterly checkups and comprehensive annual checkups to ensure that your stocks continue to meet your objectives.

✓ A rebalance, sell, or buy may be necessary at times. Discuss the tax implications of each with an advisor that you know and trust.

✓ A plethora of other means exist to monitor related economic happenings, including the Conference Board's Leading Economic Index®, the St. Louis Fed's Financial Stress Index, and Bloomberg.

STEP 10: CONTINUE DOWN YOUR PATH TO GREATNESS

Think about where you started.

You didn't have a plan to get from today to your ideal destination lifestyle. You probably didn't have a stock research process.

You definitely didn't have the Modern Wealth Media workbook, which provides support for every step of the buying stocks online process from developing a budget to building a portfolio.

Now that you have the tools, continue to search for investments and sharpen your techniques to improve your portfolios. Over the long-term, you may end up on that beach that you could only dream about not too long ago.

Please don't feel bad if you didn't understand everything the first time you read through the book. If you understood everything, you probably didn't need the book in the first place.

If you didn't understand everything, know that it takes pressure and hard times to create a diamond. Don't give up on the process until you've allowed yourself a chance to sparkle.

Okay, enough with the touchy-feely talk. Reread the book if you have to, or continue on with your journey towards developing your personal investment research and management strategy.

Don't forget to document and test everything. And if you're ever stuck, please reach out to an advisor that you trust.

Most importantly, enjoy the process! You're doing something for yourself, your family, and your future. So be proud of yourself. I'm proud of you. Thank you for reading.

HOW TO REACH THE

AUTHOR

Please share this book with your friends and family. Teach them how to reach a goal with investments. You will lift them up, their family, and future generations.

Please also speak with your local bookstore, neighborhood church, library, or university about getting this book. Everyone *needs* to know this information. Start a financial empowerment movement in your city today.

My firm, Price Capital, helps individuals invest towards their goals. We also provide excellent 401K plans for businesses.

Email: michelle.price@modernwealthmedia.com

Business Website: http://www.pricecapitalcorp.com

Personal Blog: http://www.thewallstreetgeek.com

Twitter: http://twitter.com/wallstreetgeek

Publisher's Website: http://www.modernwealthmedia.com

Contacting me does not create an advisory relationship, and I cannot dispense investment advice unless you are a client.

INDEX

Made in the USA
Lexington, KY
15 February 2019